KASHMIRI PANDITS
Violence Exodus and Reconstruction

KASHMIRI PANDITS

Violence Exodus and Reconstruction

T. N. Pandit

Pathak Publisher and Distributors
New Delhi (INDIA)

Kashmiri Pandits: Violence Exodus and Reconstruction

Author : T. N. Pandit

ISBN : 978-93-91952-08-2

Price : 1295/-

First Edition: 2024

Published by :
PATHAK PUBLISHER AND DISTRIBUTORS
E-6/33c & 34, Ground Floor, Sangam Vihar
New Delhi-110080
E-mail: pathakppd@gmail.com

An Imprint of "Research India Press"

Type Setting by
G. R. Sharma

Printed in India

Dedicated to

the Daughters of Kashmir

who walked through the Dark Night

with grace and dignity

CONTENTS

Promode Kumar Misra
Retired Professor of Anthropology,
N.E.H. University, Shillong

Mysore
July 15, 2023

FOREWORD

Triloki Nath Pandit is a dear and esteemed friend of long standing. I am honoured that he has asked me to write a foreword for his latest book based on the survey that he conducted. In that sense it is an authentic account of the saddest misery thrust upon the Kashmiri Pandits in their own home land where they excelled in almost all fields. They have been engaged in pursuit of learning, music, service to state and imparting spiritual and temporal guidance to the people. Such a peace loving and gentle community becoming a target for brutal violence will ever remain an enigma for thinkers.

I am a bit surprised that Triloki has done this book! Yes, I sincerely mean it. Triloki is a soft hearted and sensitive person, loves music, nature and writes poetry. He has his circle of friends, and admirers, and is known for his warm hospitality. He is a loveable romantic person. Above all he has spent long years in Andaman Islands, where you are struck by vastness of sea and its endlessness where you are bound to become a bit philosophical if not completely overwhelmed by spirituality. As if this was not enough he is one of the fewest persons in this world who has spent longest time with the rarest of rare people on this planet whom we civilized people prefer to call 'primitive', forest dwellers 'needing development' etc., all pejorative words for the people whose history goes back to at least sixty thousands years. They are not caught by the bug of expansion or accumulation. They live in peace with themselves, with their environment and do not harm anyone. They joyously share what they forage or hunt and when 'not working' men, women, children, merrily sing, dance or create stories and heartily laugh. They certainly admire beauty and are also given to abstract thinking. They fashion simple ornaments and wear them to enhance their looks. Even if you have spent a fraction of time with them of what Triloki has done, you will come back a transformed person and wonder what has gone wrong with the so called civilized who in their pursuit to dominate and control nature but also fellow human beings for which there is no 'Lakshman Rekha'. They literally can go to any extent. The history of mankind on this planet provides innumerable instances. While human mind has made fabulous achievements and positive vibes, evil side of it has also prospered. Science has granted men tremendous power which can bring prosperity to all but can also be used for abuse of 'others'. Who is this 'other'. It could be your neighbour who looks a little different or has different practices and beliefs or some differences are invented. The evil in human beings would like to eliminate the 'other' whom he keeps on locating and creating. I hope by now it must have become clear as to why I am surprised that Triloki has done this book. His own family and close kin are among the victims.

The story of mass exodus of the Kashmiri Pandits makes you at once to confront with the ugly and evil in human beings. Just a few pages will hit you like a thunderbolt that whatever position you may take one thing has remained constant with the human beings and that is committing violence against 'other' human beings. On this, I can do no better than quote Triloki himself 'throughout the world across the ages, human beings and human societies and cultures have vainly stressed against the sharp duality of human nature; to seek the path of peace and compassion in human affairs and at the same time to indulge in action of violence and cruelty towards fellow human beings for causes and concerns invented and nurtured by themselves and to draw satisfaction and pleasure out of such violence. No animal species has shown such enormous propensity for self-destruction.'

This is a book based on the survey of the Kashmiri Pandits who were driven out of their homes and go to refugee camps in Jammu, Kashmir Valley and Delhi. Violence against Kashmiri Pandits which began in 1986 continued reached its climax in 1990, and led to their mass exodus in 1989-90. All the data necessary to understand the plight, misery and human tragedy has been systematically provided by the author which certainly should help people to understand and introspect deeply about the extent of all out damage done.

Triloki is a well-known anthropologist of the country. He served as the Director of the Anthropological Survey of India, the premier anthropological institute of the country where he conducted and guided many significant anthropological researches in different parts of the country. His research outputs have been substantial and have been published in reputed journals and magazines. He has 6 books to his credit. His research work and statements on the indigenous people of Andaman and Nicobar Islands are read and heard with lot of respect and attention all over the world. National Geographic did a film on Triloki's work under his guidance and New York Times published his account of the indigenous people of the islands, after on interview with him in Delhi (2017).

The present book has been done in a typical anthropological fashion. It has 13 chapters complete with relevant data, references and index. Though the topic of research evokes strong reactions, Triloki has remained true to his training in anthropology and has allowed his data as collected from the field to speak. The book presents a brief history of Kashmir, a profile of the Kashmiri Pandits, genesis of exodus and an account of loss of property and lives. Forceful uprooting of people from their homes and hearths is a tragedy for the survivors beyond description. How the Kashmir Pandits are coping up with the tragedy in the new environment of relief camps have been objectively provided. In particular I would like to underline this aspect. Triloki himself is a Kashmiri Pandit. His near and close relatives have been victims of this holocaust yet he has presented an objective report which is remarkable but must have caused a tremendous tension to him.

There is one very conspicuous aspect of this man made tragedy. Violence against the Kashmir Pandits began in 1986 which continued and reached its ugly climax in 1990. Surprisingly there was not much hue and cry about it. There was no serious and dedicated urgent action by the concerned authorities both in State and Central Governments to protect them from holocaust. The attitude of the political parties and media was generally muted. Further the people with whom the Kashmiri Pandits shared their habitats for centuries 'preferred to remain silent and saw the happenings with an unseeing eye'. It is not difficult to state that the perpetrators of the crime to say the least found the Kashmiri Pandits as soft target but what about the authorities whose prime responsibility was to provide safety and protection to its citizens particularly those who were the most vulnerable. That guilt would be difficult to wipe out.

Kashmir has ancient and luminous history and has been home to several spiritual schools and philosophy. It is well known for its scenic beauty and has been termed as paradise on the earth. Its soulful music, arts and crafts are famous all over the world. Its lofty hills may challenge human spirit but also have been centres of the Hindu pilgrimage. The evil and greed nurtured in some human minds have led to splurging of the innocent blood on such a sacred and peaceful land which certainly would not go away in a hurry. This book should prick the conscience of those who chose to remain silent while this gory act was being committed.

Promode Kumar Misra
Retired Professor of Anthropology,
North Eastern Hill University, Shillong

ACKNOWLEDGEMENTS

We gratefully acknowledge the valued assistance and cooperation of the following ladies and gentlemen in the execution and completion of the Research Project and this Report:

Dr. Satyabhama Razdan, Head of the Department of Linguistics & Sanskrit, Kashmir University was of immense help in arrangements for fieldwork in Kashmir Valley. Ajay Zutshi visited the distant villages and towns there for data collection. His contribution was most valuable. Ramesh Bhat and late M. L. Kaul made the arrangements for fieldwork in Jammu and Nagrota migrant camps. Sarojini Pandit took the entire responsibility for organising fieldwork in Udhampur town and camps. Good and timely work was done with their help.

We were very happy to get the services of three young research scholars from Anthropology Department, Delhi University: Abhilasha Mishra, Kajri Tandon, and Shilpi Gupta. They worked as my research assistants in the Project. They helped in various academic discussions and collection of data in Delhi. Abhilasha Mishra also worked in the later phases of the Project and assisted me in library work, data analysis and chapter arrangements. Naina Pandit has assisted me in data arrangements and making notes for report writing and proof reading of the typed material.

Rukshana Zaman another research scholar in anthropology at Delhi University, jointly with M/s Binary Systems took care of data entry and tabulation work etc. for the Project.

I am grateful to M. K. Kaw for accepting my request to be the Project Director of the Project and reading through the Draft Report.

Chandra Shekhar Singh, erstwhile librarian of KECSS, has been of great help in arranging and typing out the draft report and the final report along with about forty tables using all his computer skills in the process.

I am much indebted to Lal Chand Kaul, a highly respected member of the KECSS, for his keen concern for the success of the Project and for his periodic assistance with valuable information relevant to this Report.

Thanks are due to J. N. Kaul (President), J. L. Bhatt (General Secretary), S. N. Kaul (Vice President), Arun Shalia (Vice President), B. B. Dhar (erstwhile Vice President), Anil Shakdhar (Treasurer), Vinod Kaul (erstwhile Treasurer), and Vinod Yadav (Accountant) of the KECSS for their interest and general assistance in the work of the Project.

Finally, I wish to express my deep gratitude to all the KP migrant families - men, women and children - covered under this study, for their ungrudging cooperation, kind hospitality and cordial attitude shown to our investigators.

T. N. Pandit

PREFACE

We in the KECSS had for the last few years felt the urgent need for a properly researched report on the uprooted Kashmiri Pandits following their mass exodus from Kashmir Valley in 1989-90, as no such study was available — published or unpublished.

Our research proposal submitted to the Department of Women and Child Development, Govt. of India in 2001 received prompt and serious consideration and a grant of Rs 4,24,000/- was sanctioned for this Project. We express our gratitude to them for this timely grant, which has made this report possible.

The strength and value of this report is because of it being based on factual data collected by canvassing a schedule and the interviews held with individuals affected directly by the militancy. It is not a report based on any published material or hypothetical assumptions. Our aim is to present the actual situation on the ground before the readers. The basic data has been collected by our enthusiastic young men and women through a door-to-door survey undertaken in various parts of Delhi, Jammu, and difficult locations in Kashmir Valley.

Another aspect of this report is that we have taken utmost care to keep it on an objective plane. It is often seen that reports or studies are biased, either due to some prejudices or due to some political or economic considerations. But we are happy to state that no such consideration has influenced our presentation. Chapter 9 of this report is exclusively devoted to some concise statements recorded in the field during the survey. These original statements have been reproduced without any comment for their proper impact.

T. N. Pandit

KASHMIR : THE HOMELAND

and

PROLOGUE : THE KASHMIR STORY

KASHMIR THE HOMELAND

Amidst the high Himalayas
there was the lake Satisar.
Rishi Kashyap prayed to Shiv Shankar.
He cut open the western Hills and drained the excess water.
Kashmir Valley was then revealed in all its green glory.
That was the start of a long story
Gods and goddesses blessed the land
and let things happen as destiny planned.

Our earliest ancestors came here in stone age times.
They lived in homes like at Burz-home.
Over thousands of years people came here from far and near.

Huns and Kushans, Mongols and Turks, Persians and
Uzbeks, Panjabis and Pathans.
They exchanged genes, customs and cultures that made a
happy mix of happy things.
Maharaja Ashok talked of "Budhas Middle Path",
Maharaja Kanishk brought in the reminder.
Aadi Shankar held fourth on Vedant and Maya.
Abhinav Gupt sang in devotion to Param Shiva.
For Soofi saints it was sheer bliss to chant for grace of Allah,
Allah hoo, Allah hoo.
And believe in Brotherhood of Humanity at large.
Saint-poet Lal Ded expressed her philosophy in "Lal Vakhs"
Nund Rishi joined the proceedings with Soofi "Trukhs".

Kalhana wrote "Rajtarangini" The Story of Hindu Kings.
Lalitadityas empire extended to Central Asia.
He built the famous Martand Temple.
Five centuries of Muslim rule passed through periods of Sultans, Mughals and Afghan rule.
Great Sultan Zainul-Abidin called back KPs. driven out by Sultan Sikandar, his father.
Mughal Royals loved Kashmir deeply Akbar built the fort Hari Parbat.
Jahangir and Shahjahan laid out lovely gardens.
Maharaja Ranjit Singh annexed Kashmir ending the Afghan rule.
Dogra Raj commenced in 1846 and lasted for a century of peace and harmony.
Then came Acesession and era of "Awami Raj"
Peace restored with ceasefire after Indo-Pak War.
Farmers sang Haba Khatoon's songs in rice fields.
Poets Mahjoor, Zinda Kaul, Prakash Ram, Azad, Nadim sang about life, love, nature and matters spiritual.
But then more wars happened with China in 1962,
with Pakistan in 1965, 1971 and Bangladesh was born.
And things started warming up in Kashmir.
A blood-thirsty "nose-cut" went about dancing in the Valley.
Soon the air and earth and water of Vitasta turned red
with the blood of the innocent, then EXODUS.
The joyful sound of Sitar and Santoor fell silent.
Jackals kept howling in empty spaces, and owls kept watch over dark nights.
But thank heavens peace has returned to the Valley.
The odd incidents are just warning signals against any major action in aid of K.Ps return.
Let Future work out its own mystique and mechanisms.

(adapted from the original Kashmiri)

PROLOGUE: THE KASHMIR STORY

The present study was written in 2005 and is based on data generated in 2002-2003 Till now it was available only in limited circulation. But now we decided that the book deserves proper publication and easy accessbility as a document of much value in this tragic story. The basic strength of this study is that it reflects the ground level reality as perceived by the victims themselves thirteen years after the EXODUS. The chapter on "Nadimarg Massacre" is a case of special reportage. I personally interviewed a senior resident of the village and recorded all the details soon after the tragic incident had occurred.

It is now almost two decades since the above study was done. What has changed in this long period apart from the demographic factors? The entire migrant population has continued to pursue the path of reconstruction as well as possible by investing in children's education and exerting to garner economic resources, whichever way, to improve and stabilise their life condition – reportedly quite a good number have achieved notable success in their efforts. Some relief measures covering registered migrants like salaries drawn got converted to pensions and pensions reached their conclusion with death. Some families have exited the relief aid either voluntarily or for technical reasons. But of course government relief measures of whatever kind – residence, cash, rations etc – have contributed to the survival of the recepients under distressing circumstances. However the sad reality that confronts the Indian nation is the inability of the Kashmiri pandit community to reclaim their roots and life in their homeland, Kashmir valley. Thirty-three years have gone by since The EXODUS and we are still waiting for the hopes and repeated assurances to translate into reality! Will they or will they not? The answer lies in the in depth analysis of the situation. We will make an effort to do that.

Kulgam: District Town

Let me describe my credentials for getting involved with this vital subject and writing this report. First and foremost I am a Kashmiri, a Kashmiri speaking Kashmiri and also a Kashmiri Pandit born and brought up and educated in Kashmir.

I was born in a well educated K.P. family with a liberal and humane outlook. I also happen to be a student of human behavior as an anthropologist. Besides, while growing up in Kashmir I was able to observe at close range the kind of cordiality that informed the relations between the K.Ps. and the Muslim brotherhood Living there. I was naturally a participant in the dynamics of the inter community relations and interaction. I spent 8 years at Kulgam with my grandparents and attended the local middle school there. Kulgam, the tehsil headquarter with a rural-urban ambience, was a haven of peaceful existence in the forties of the last century. There was no electricity and water was available only from running streams, and springs for daily requirements. Of course the town itself is situated on the banks of a big river Vishav a tributary of river Jhelum.

Growing up here it was easy to observe that for all kinds of services needed in daily life, K.Ps were entirely dependent on the Muslim professional workers, Barber and Butcher, Cobbler and Carpenter, Weaver and Woodcutter, Potter and Plumber, Mason and Mazdoor (labourer), Darzi (Tailor) and Dhobi (washerman) Peasant and Cowherd and so on. The basic fact is that during the centuries of Muslim rule in Kashmir, all the occupational groups lower down in the caste hierarchy got converted to Islam. The only Hindus left out were a part of The K.P. population. And the only work the latter were traditionally required and inclined to do were priesthood and religious teaching, school and office jobs and running general shops etc. These jobs needed education and did not involve any heavy manual or "unsuitable" kind of work. But of course, K.Ps. utilized all the services as required and made available by their Muslim brothers. Services were paid for in cash and kind as per availability of resources and mutual arrangements. The relationship of K.Ps with Muslims at various levels were very cordial based on mutual need and mutual respect. There was recognition and acceptance of the fact that all communities whether Hindu or Muslim were but segments of the larger Kashmiri society with shared biological origins going back to eternity. And then there was thousands of years of common prehistory, history, culture and language. These concepts and beliefs were implied not shouted about. They flowed with the current of daily life like the cool breeze on a spring morning. The well off K.Ps. would arrange a special feast for the Muslim neighbours after a wedding in the family. My family followed this practice even in the sixties of the last century. I still remember the names of some of my Muslim classmates – Yasin, Yusuf, Qasim, Mubarak, Ghaffar – at Govt. Middle School Kulgam, who taught me to recite the "Kalma". the Muslim prayer which I remember even now. The memory gives me a nostalgic feeling about the good old days! That is how things were then. The term " Kashmiryat ", created much later, should be inclusive of all the positive elements that defined life then.

Kashmir "Problem"

In the British ruled India, Jammu and Kashmir had been areawise the largest and highly strategically located princely state in the country. Its boarders touched Tibet(China), India and Pakistan (after August 15,1947) and were not far from Afghanistan and some central Asian countries. The hundred years of Dogra rule over the state (1846-1947) was one of peace and tranquility. There were no conflicts and wars and even the crime rate was very low. Jammu and Kashmir was one of the better administered princely states in the country. Maharaja Hari Singh was a ruler with a modernistic outlook and a life style unencumbered by any extraordinary feudalistic idiosyncracies. There was always a cabinet headed by a distinguished personage as Prime Minister. A high court was maintained as an important functional unit of the state. There also used to be an assembly elected by popular vote. Then there was the well trained army, limited to a force of 10,000, under British orders. This army had actively participated in both the world wars but in 1947 it was not in a position in terms of numbers, equipment, management and preparedness – to defend the state against the Pakistani attack. That put an end to the maharaja's rule and shaped the history of the Indian subcontinent in a very negative way. Had Maharaja of Kashmir signed "The Instrument of Accession" with the Indian union well before October 22, 1947. Pakistan would not have dared to attack the state, However, these are the " ifs and buts" of history. But the attack did happen and it impacted the future developments in the history and politics of the Indian subcontinents in a far reaching way. For the state of Jammu and Kashmir for Kashmir Valley especially it had ushered in an era of prolonged conflict and violence. Peace was restored in 1949 through the U.N. imposed cease-fire agreement. Indo-Pak wars happened again in 1965, 1971 (Bangladesh), and 1999 (Kargil). In 1962 there was Indo-Chinese war affecting Ladakh and the North eastern

Himalayan region of India. The prolonged freedom struggle of India led by Mahatma Gandhi had been expressly peaceful and non-violent but freedom came to partitioned India amidst huge amounts of blood letting and disruption of lives of millions of Hindus, Muslims and Sikhs throughout the sub-continent, And to crown it all, the rulers of newly born Pakistan decided to attack the hapless Jammu and Kashmir state eventually leading to several wars and prolonged conflict with the newly independent sister nation i.e. India. After the first Indo-Pak war of 1947-48 itself something basic changed about the ambience the word "Kashmir" conveyed earlier i.e. a naturally most beautiful and peaceful place on earth. After the first and the subsequent wars the term "Kashmir dispute" conveys the rich meaning of its potential for endangering peace between the big nuclear powered nations in Asia. That could further threaten world peace and world order. In a way the aura and charm of natural beauty and peace and tranquility that informed the erstwhile state of Jammu and Kashmir and Ladakh earlier are since being held hostage to the war- ridden atmosphere of Indo-Pak Kashmir Dispute and Indo-China Border Dispute. The pictures of fully equipped rival armies facing each other in eye-ball to eye ball confrontation along the lines of control/borders, impacts the peoples imagination regarding war-related violence and its far reaching consequences. These have the potential to provide a contextual pretext for use of different violent instruments for achieving objectives of a contrary kind e.g. terrorism. We will revert to this subject a little later. In the mean time, we shall have a closer look at the developments in the J and K state in Kashmir Valley especially transforming the life of people at large in a drastic manner.

Kashmir "Dispute"

With the Kashmir case repeatedly coming alive on the agenda of the U.N. Security Council after the Pakistani attack in October 1947, it acquired the dubious status (for India) of a great INTERNATIONAL DISPUTE which opened the door for other countries and international press to eriticise India. The Pakistani case was quite simple, India had been partitioned on the basis of Hindu / Muslim majority areas constituting India/Pakistan respectively. And J and K being a Muslim majority state should have gone to Pakistan. But the ground reality and Indian stand regarding the Kashmir situation has been more complex. However, irrespective of all wars and various claims made on either side, both India and Pakistan have jointly maintained the ceasefire agreement across the "line of control" in the J and K state area, between wars. Accordingly the original territory of the J and K state under Maharaja's rule remains divided between "Indian Kashmir" and "Pakistan occupied Kashmir" (POK)- Besides, China is in occupation of part of the Ladakh Region. Thus Pakistan and China are both in illegal control of big chunks of territory of J & K state as it was in 1947 under The Maharaja's rule. In a way China and Pakistan are both happy to be creating trouble for India in this area. China is doing so elsewhere also in the name of the "Border Dispute" along the Himalayas in the central and eastern regions. Apart from waging wars Pakistan has been indulging in other kinds of destructive activities in J & K to disrupt and weaken India's association with it.

And Terrorism

Kashmir has been in the eye of the storm since October 1947 when Pakistan attacked the state the first time and other wars followed later. But wars apart Pakistan has been causing trouble by subjecting the people of the state-especially those in the Kashmir Valley – to poisonous propaganda through all media, preaching to religious gatherings in mosques etc, and brainwashing of youth and targeted individuals. Thematically the propaganda was anti India like Muslims not being treated well in Hindu India. Much effort was devoted to radicalize the soft Soofi Islam widely practiced and followed by Kashmiri Muslims. This was the kind of Islam, that as a vital element of the centuries old tradition of mutual acceptance and togetherness, found resonance with the utterly peaceful and softly ritualistic Shaivite Hinduism practiced by Kashmiri Pandits. This was part of what Kashmiriat was all about. Pakistan needed to change all that and towards that objective, to communalise The Kashmir Valley into an aggressive and militant Islamic society that can produce volunteers for violent activity (terrorism) at the risk of even losing their own lives (and "earn a place in jannat" heaven. To achieve the above objectives, Pakistan has had a long term plan which has been operationalised through various stages as per circumstances. Pakistan's Interservices Intelligence (ISI) is and has been in charge of all the planning, organization and resource mobilization for all the subversive work in Kashmir. It took decades of efforts for Pakistan to get the desired response at various stages of their campaign from a section of the people in the Valley. Initially it was luke warm, then it became warm and the intensity of thought processes manifested itself in the creation of openly pro-Pakistan outfits advocating Nizam-e-Mustafa (Rule under Islamic Law), merger with Pakistan and armed rebellion against India. The unemployed and the unemployable angry youngmen became stone pelting and gun wielding militants, quite often in defiance of the advice of their families, The intense presence of security forces with wide powers to search, surround and confront people and places on suspicion, and the J & K police personnel keeping track of the subversive elements, were both highly resented by the latter. So these institutions had to be targeted for violent action. At some point the various anti India outfits with slogans like "Azadi". Rai Shumari (referendum)", "Pakistan" etc. joined forces to charge up the atmosphere through slogan shouting processions and gatherings in the mosques etc. Also the list of "undesirable" persons kept increasing. Even anger with respect to routine administrative matters would be added to the anti India sentiment. The happenings in India like Punjab militancy and Babri-Masjid demolition and its aftermath, and growth of Taliban in Pakistan and Afghanistan, civil war in Sri Lanka and "Ayat-ullah revolution" in Iran must have fired the imagination of the militants and also of the Pakistani planners. So the tension in The Kashmir Valley had to be raised to the highest pitch to provide a fertile ground for major action there. Hence all pro-India people, officials, liberal minded persons had to be eliminated. Exploratory work was carried out in the eighties of the last century by networking and spreading the word across the countryside and small towns about future action plan. "Narco-terrorism" was introduced by Pakistan to add to and aid in the destructive work being done in The Valley. It affected the local Kashmiri population very badly on account of spread of drug addiction among the youth.

Violence and Exodus

As the situation was heating up towards open lawlessness, rumour mongering, threats and acts of violence and armed insurrection, the state government then headed by Farooq Abdullah was deeply stressed about how to deal with the anarchic situation. The central government was then headed by V.P. Singh and his Home Minister was Mufti Mohd. Sayeed.

In 1986 some Hindu temples were damaged and shops looted in Anantnag district. During 1987-89 the language of hate became more virulent and wide spread nurturing threats and acts of violence across The Valley.

In July 1988 JKLF (Jammu and Kashmir Liberation Front) made an open declaration of separatist insurgency. And on September 14, 1989, Tika Lal Taploo, a Kashmiri Pandit, an advocate and president BJP, was shot dead by a JKLF man in Srinagar within days another well known K.P., justice Ganju, was also killed in the same manner while he was walking in The Hari Singh High Street, Srinagar. Soon the news of sporadic incidents changed to large scale violence involving random and targeted killings of K.P. men and women. Extreme fear and anxiety gripped the collective mind of the K.P. community. The upshot was the Exodus, the sudden and panic induced departure of hundreds of thousands of K.Ps, leaving behind their homes and hearths and seeking safety and shelter across Banihat Tunnel – the exit point from Kashmir Valley.

Well history had taken a reverse step by repeating itself after five and a half centuries. It was during the rule of Sultan Sikandar (1398-1413) that the K.Ps. were subjected to cruelties their temples destroyed and most of their population had to leave Kashmir and go and live in other regions in India. But his son, Sultan Zainul Abadin (1420-1470) proved to be a noble king. During his 50 year rule he was able to bring back a good number of K.Ps and help them settle down in Kashmir again.

However, today 33 years after the EXODUS, we K.Ps. have not been able to return to our homeland. There is no great king Zainul who will work the magic and apply the balm of happy togetherness to help reconstruct the benign state of Kashmiriat – segments rediscovering each other to make the real whole.

After Exodus

Around mid – January 1990 Jagmohan took charge as Governor of J & K state and Farook Abdullha resigned some day as Chief Minister. The state assembly was dissolved and president's rule declared. At This time the state was administratively in a real mess. The valley was in turmoil with the militant violence, EXODUS, and angry protestors reacting to heavy casualties caused by the action of the security forces in Srinagar and Jammu was aghast with the thousands of hapless K.Ps. pouring in from the Valley day and night Governor announced urgent relief measures for the uprooted K.Ps. in Jammu, Delhi etc. They were now called MIGRANTS, obviously a misnomer. In reality they were IDPs (Internally Displaced Persons). Jagmohan had the tough job to awaken and shake up the listless state administration to function effectively for bringing peace and normalcy to life here – amidst the ambience of violence, disruptions and mayhem.

The data and information presented in the ensuing chapters are based on a survey conducted by me in 2002-2003 covering 743 K.P. migrant families in Delhi, Jammu and Kashmir. That was 13 years after The Exodus. The initial three years were nightmarish. But gradually they were making every effort to marshall their meager resources and keep confronting the situation head on. The goal of Reconstruction had three obvious priorities on the path of peaceful progress namely:

(a) Survival - basic needs of food, shelter etc

(b) Health care including hospitalization facility

(c) Education of children school, college, professional

As time passed the migrant K.Ps. were able to progressively access their priorities as per their needs and choice – not in one go most of the time but one area or the other. The situation as it was in 2002-2003 is reflected in the following chapters. That is the picture 13 years after EXODUS. Since then another 20 years have come through. So today 33 years after leaving Kashmir the life conditions of the migrants have vastly improved with lot of exposure to the wider world. The wider exposure enabled the young boys and girls to explore more and good educational opportunities to compete in the job market. The girls education has received special impetus because of available facilities and for their need to work outside home. The overall flavor is one of optimism on the path of reconstruction of life post EXODUS. But Kashmir remains distant as ever.

Situation Today – July 2023

(A) ARTICLE 370: The most important change that has been brought in here by the govt. of India is of a constitutional nature with wide ranging political implications. In August 2019, after abrogation of the Article 370 of the constitution granting J & K state a special status, the state was divided into two Union Territories (U.Ts) of Ladakh and J and K. Each U.T. has since been administered by a Lt. Governor. All elections and state Legislatures remain suspended. The petitions questioning the move are currently being heard by a five judge bench of the Supreme Court of India. Downgrading the status of a constituent state of the Union (Republic) by converting it into a couple of U.Ts. directly administered by the Home Ministry does not sound a wonderful idea! But it is a temporary measure.

(B) RETURN OF K.PS.: Whatever the migrant KPs. might have gained or lost following The EXODUS, their desire for re-claiming their home in their homeland in Kashmir Valley has remained supreme in their mind and heart. But their wish has eluded them even 33 years after their exile.

Many promises and expectations have been of no avail as the terrorist outfits want the valley to remain a purely Muslim area. They are creating fear through selective targeted killings of the non – Muslims especially KPs. in local public offices and elsewhere.

However, Govt. of India, in its recent submission to the Supreme Court, has conveyed its cautious optimism regarding the completion in about a year's time, the "work on the transit accommodation for Kashmiri Pandits for their safe return to the Valley". This of course will only be the first stage of the huge project of "Rehabilitation of K.Ps. in their Homeland" The issue is very complex with political, physical, social, cultural, psychological, economic and financial implications. All these factors have to blend in a manner that positive action becomes possible. And there is always the fear of the terrorists responding in scale to the size of the advance parties of KPs returning to the Valley. Right now these suppositions and questions are hypothetical but can be anticipated realistically.

However, right now the situation is weighed down with 'if' and 'but' and 'when' and 'how' and the uncertainties of the future. A little poem of mine reflects the situation succinctly.

Shadows

The shadows of silence
But reflect
the cadences of the past rhythms.
And the present hangs heavy
Like a wet canopy.
dripping ambiguities.
But who knows
What the future holds
In the velvet folds

Of its womb
One lives on fantasies
Licking droplets
Of vapourised hope!!

So, let the matter rest here for now and believe that whatever will be, will be for the best.

Demography-Change (1990-2023)

The EXODUS of the K.Ps. from The Valley happened in 1989-90. Now the children born across the period of the last 33 years both in the Valley and in the K.P. community constitute about 45% of the population on either side. About 28% of the total population is constituted by 15 to 30+ age grades on either side.

The important conclusion is that these most active and vibrant sections of the population on either side have had no opportunity to know each other as next door neighbours in towns and distant villages in Kashmir Valley. Their knowledge and opinion about each other as communities is second hand, based on what they have heard from their respective elders. But irrespective of this deficiency in terms of the existing realities, it is the segment of respective communities that will condition and influence the future course of action in the state. May God grant all concerned plenty of wisdom and compassion and may the atmosphere there resonate with thoughts of peace and prosperity.

Kashmiriat - What Now?

In 1946-1947, among several hundred princely states, Jammu and Kashmir was unique in several respects, Areawise it was the largest with three well defined regions namely Kashmir

Valley. Jammu region and Ladakh region. Each region had its distinct geography, history, culture, language and predominant religion. Predominantly Kashmiris are Muslims, Jammu people are Hindus and Ladakhis are Buddhists. The state had borders touching India, Pakistan (newly created) and China (Tibet). Also it had close historical and cultural ties with Iran, Afghanistan and some central Asian countries. After August 15, 1947 Maharaja of Jammu and Kashmir (and Ladakh) hesitated in taking a quick decision regarding accession. But with Pakistani attack on October 22, 1947, history took care of itself. In 1962 China also joined the party by waging war against India and illegally occupying a huge chunk of territory in Ladakh.

And Pakistan has already been in control of about one third of the area of the original Jammu province of the state. But The Valley of Kashmir has remained completely under Indian control as part of the Indian Union. As a Muslim dominated area the Valley has been the hub of the dispute with Pakistan. In this context the Indo-Pakistan wars happened in 1947-48. 1965 and 1971 without causing any communal violence against Hindu (K.Ps.) minority. That happened two decades later (1989-90).

Martand Temple

Kashmiriat is not just a pretty sounding word it is a historically lived concept that informed and sustained the deeply felt positive outlook in Kashmiri culture and society, for five and a half centuries. Sultan Zainul Abadin had during his 50 year (1420-1470) rule, restored peaceful conditions and a sense of brotherhood between the Hindus (K.Ps) and Muslims in Kashmir and was nurtured by his just and benign rule. He thus succeeded in undoing the serious damage that had been done to the ethos and composition of the Kashmiri society by the destructive and anti-Hindu policies followed by his father Sultan Sikandar (1398-1413). During his violent misrule KPs were obliged to abandon their homes in Kashmir to live elsewhere in India. The atrocities they faced included large scale destruction of Hindu temples including the famous Martand Temple near Anantang built by the great Emperor Lalitaditya in the 8th Century. Sikandar carried out his destructive work with venomous zeal and personally participated in demolition and desecration of many temples but the magnificent Martand Temple (dedicated to the Sun god) is said to have received his special attention. This must have been for obvious reasons. Martand was not just a large and popular temple. It must have been for Kashmiris all through the centuries the celebrated monument to a great creative effort in terms of the unique concept, location, materials, architecture and engineering a marvel to be ever proud of The glorious Matand Temple, even today in its ruins, remains majestic and awesome as a structure of unique architectural beauty and spiritual ambience. Many years ago, I had an opportunity to visit the site. Watching the temple in silence I kept breathing in the serene atmosphere. In a while I heard the sonorous sound of chanting of sacred mantras. Also in the background was the gentle splash of river Lidar flowing down stream in homage to Surya-Dev. Surya Dev then rose up from behind the Himalayas and lighted up the Sky and the Earth and, of course, the Martand Temple. The places of worship and prayer are sacred places and they remain consecrated in the hearts of the devotees for ever and ever!

Recently on two occasions groups of people one led by the *Lt. Governor Sinha* himself-offered pooja at Martand. A matter of deep sentiment!

Sultan Sikandar, in terms of his violence laden policies against the Kashmiri Hindus (K.Ps.) violated the basic teaching of Islam of protecting the innocent. And todays militants in Kashmir in their temptation to indulge in violent heroics have been promoting themselves to the category of "TERRORISTS". The culture of terrorism is killing the innocent. That is how K.Ps. were forced to leave Kashmir and their homes and hearts. To Pakistan goes the credit of long term planning and guidance and material and human support to the growth and operations of TERRORISM in Kashmir. It is also called "CROSS-BORDER TERRORISM" in international media and diplomatic parlance.

Another gift of Pakistan to Kashmiris is what is termed as "Narco-Terrorism". As per official estimates about 13 lakh people, mostly youth in the Valley, have become drug-dependent edicts in the state the unofficial estimates are even higher.

Kashmir Valley has been a well defined geographical area and the people living here for thousands of years, over time evolved into an integrated Kashmiri Society sustained by common language and inclusive culture. This situation remained stable and reaffirmed itself after occasional setbacks caused by man made or natural disasters. Deep faith in life of cordial and constructive togetherness across caste class and religion in good times and bad, is what Kashmiriat has been all about. Obviously the day a Kashmiri Muslim killed a K.P. simply because he was a Hindu, he attacked also the idea and reality of Kashmiriat. The rest was history in the making!

Kashmir our Homeland

The uprooted people anywhere in the world pine for returning to their homes and homeland. So we Kashmiri Pandits have been patiently waiting for the official arrangements for our safe return and rehabilitation in Kashmir. But due to complexities of the situation govt. of India has not been able to take any major steps in this direction. Now 33 years after the Exodus, the dream of reclaiming their place in Kashmir Valley, for the K.Ps, seems to be stretching beyond reach. The basic question is of safety and security as terrorists continue to target security forces and non-Muslims from time to time as a "message of disapproval". So the "terrorist hurdle" needs to be eliminated for further progress in this project!

I have visited Kashmir a few times post 1990 in 2002, 2003, 2007, 2017 and Jammu also a couple of times. Had the chance to interact with a cross section of people-univeristy teachers, shalwalas, shikarawalas govt. officials college girls shopkeepers, hotel staff, taxi drivers almost all of them Kashmiri Mulsims. Everyone was so polite and cordial. But the sad moments came when I went to see our old home in Srinagar. In its place there was an ugly structure. However, visiting Kulgam, my birth place, was a matter of deeply felt emotion and sentiment as I had spent all my childhood years here with my grandparents and uncless and away from my own parents and siblings. In fact I had attended local school here till class eight. From Srinagar we-self and a friend came over in a jeep, courtery a local official. At Kulgam we were hosted warmly by a kind and courteous local resident who happened to know my family well. Our old home, an imposing four storeyed red brick structure, had been partially burnt years back. Just went to see the site. All that I saw there was a mound of mud, not a brick nor a stone or a piece of wood lying around anywhere! Well, lesson learnt once again- "all material possessions are just MAYA (illusion)".

Moved on to happier experiences offered a prayer at the temple of our own goddess "Kulwageshori". The idol-so familier was in perfect condition and the temple was being reconstructed with the support of the local Muslim brothers. Very sweet. Now, we were at the gates of my dear old "Govt. Middle School-Boys" since grown into a Senior Secondary School for Girls. A new, building was there near the old chinar trees. But the smaller older structure with three classrooms (then for classes 6, 7 and 8) and the fourth room for the Headmaster (now Principal) was very much there.

For the teachers, a youngish lot, our visit was a pleasant surprise. Five-six of them sat with us in the open, for a nice chat over a cup of tea, with an ex-student who had passed out in class 8 from here in 1947. A joyful experience. This meeting happened in 2007. By the evening we were back in Srinagar and next day we flew into Delhi. Before leaving Kulgam our gracious host told us that his own life was in danger as the local militants did not like his liberal views. Even today Kulgam remains in the news for attacks and violent encounters happening from time to time. This is 2023. Also in place of our homes in Kulgan there now stands the office complex of the Deputy Commissioner. Kulgam district, the market value of the land area taken over is in crores. For us the owners there is now no place to come back to if such a possibility arises ever.

Final Word

Human life on this planet Earth is an ongoing ever going and ever changing story. Humankind adapts to change through good times and bad and ensures its own survival and dominance here. But while we reap the benefits of good times, we wade through pain and suffering in adverse situations. We Kashmiri Pandits have gone through a cataclysmic phase which uprooted us from our homes and homeland and caused us limitless pain and misery. After paying a heavy price for being a peace loving and non-violent community, we have collectively regained our compsure to keep pursuing the path of reconstruction. Even while living hundreds and thousands of miles away from Kashmir our identity as individuals or at community level is for ever linked to it. We carry our culture language and history with us with feelings of respect and pride in our hearts. The FUTURE may have surprises in store, let it write its own grammar!

In closing this conversation, may I offer my most respectful greetings to my Kashmiri Brothers wishing them all peace and prosperity.

Namaskar, Salam, Sat Siri Akal

August 15, 2023 **T.N. Pandit**

CHAPTER – 1

INTRODUCTION

Background

Kashmir Valley has had a chequered political history both during the long rule of Hindu kings and the five centuries (1339-1827AD) of Muslim rule. There has been a lot of strife and periodic excitement, violence and destruction caused by local rebellions, change of ruling kings and dynasties, invasions from various quarters, natural and man-made calamities, coming of high voltage leaders preaching new philosophies and religious streams. These troublesome times of internecine fighting, floods and famines causing all round misery have, of course, been interspersed by benign periods of political stability, peace and all round prosperity. For instance, we would mention the names of the great kings like Lalitaditya (724-761 AD) and Avantivarman (855-883 AD) and Sultan Zainulabidin, popularly called Bud Shah (1420-1470 AD) etc. One of the two examples of the worst kings is that of king Harsha of Lohara Dynasty (1089-1101 AD), though a Hindu, ordered the desecration of Hindu temples all over Kashmir and plundered their wealth and idols and melted them to obtain gold, silver and copper for making coins and building his own wealth for his own political purposes. But his vandalism and misrule and weak character eventually led to his downfall and a miserable death. The other notable and notorious example is that of Sultan Sikandar, the idol breaker who ruled Kashmir three centuries later (1389-1413 AD). His Islamic zeal coupled with his destructive and cruel disposition made him launch a campaign to destroy Hindu temples and idols all over the Valley including the celebrated Martand Temple near Anantnag built by king Lalitaditya in the eighth century.

Emperor Akbar annexed Kashmir as part of his Mughal Empire in 1589 AD. The Mughal rule lasted for 164 years and was generally progressive and mindful of the public good and the economic development of the Valley. The Afghan ruler Ahmad Shah Abdali captured Kashmir in 1753 AD. For the next 67 years Kashmir was subjected to the most unjust, cruel and ruthless administration it had ever seen, at the hands of its Afghan rulers. Maharaja Ranjit Singh, the most powerful king in North-West India at the time annexed Kashmir as part of his kingdom in 1819 AD. The Sikh rule lasted till 1846 AD following the decisive defeat of the Sikh armies (after the death of Maharaja Ranjit Singh in 1839 AD) at the hands of the British forces. Through an agreement with the British East India Company, Gulab Singh, the Dogra ruler of Jammu took over as ruler of Kashmir also with the title of Maharaja. The Dogra rule lasted till 1947. With the departure of the British rule in India two independent states of India and Pakistan were born on August 15, 1947. The princely state of Jammu and Kashmir became part of the Indian Union with the signing of the Instrument of Accession by the Maharaja on October 26, 1947, following the armed invasion of the state by the Pakistani army and irregulars. The Indian army took over the defence of the state after the accession. The Pakistani forces were pushed back from the Valley after the war that lasted for fourteen months, till a ceasefire between Indian and Pakistani forces was declared in January 1949 under the auspices of the

United Nations. At the time of cease-fire approximately about one-third area of the state was still under the occupation of the Pakistani forces. The position remains the same today. Thus with the signing of the cease-fire agreement in 1949 by India and Pakistan was laid the foundation of a problem - the Kashmir problem — between them. This problem remains unresolved till date and this state of affairs has had vast implications for the people of India and Pakistan in general, and the people of Jammu and Kashmir, specially Kashmir Valley in particular.

Since 1947-48 India and Pakistan have fought more major wars in 1965, 1971 and 1998 (Kargil). To complicate the situation further we also had to fight a border war with China in 1962; it has been in illegal occupation of 37,555 sq. kms of our land in the Ladakh region of Jammu and Kashmir for the last half a century. Pakistan has further illegally ceded 5180 sq. Kms of land area in the state to China, illegally occupied by it since 1947.

Having failed to annex Kashmir Valley (that is the real focus of dispute) through either military means or diplomatic efforts at the United Nations and elsewhere, Pakistan has over time devised other means of weakening India's hold and strong legal and moral position on Kashmir. In 1965 it started sending trained infiltrators into the state, especially Kashmir Valley, to instigate the people against the government and cause all round destruction, violence and panic. But due to lack of response from the people of the state this experiment failed. However, since the late eighties Pakistan has launched a full scale low intensity underground war against India in Jammu and Kashmir, and elsewhere through terrorists recruited, trained and equipped by it in the so-called Azad Kashmir territory and elsewhere in Pakistan. It has also been helping and encouraging other militant and terrorist groups operating in India. Pakistan's open and active support to militancy and terrorism in Punjab (India) in the earlier decades is well-known. The Government of India has all these years been fighting terrorism and terrorists in Kashmir physically (with the help of the security forces), politically and diplomatically within the country and internationally by creating international opinion against it. At the same time it has been engaging the Pakistan government and various leaders of political opinion in Kashmir to sort out all issues centred round the so called Kashmir problem and the establishment of durable peace in the subcontinent. By now (close of September 2005) we have made some visible progress and the efforts are on to gain greater momentum towards achieving concrete results in the above objectives.

The Exodus

During the mid eighties - specifically 1986 onwards - the secessionists, pro-Pakistan and anti Indian elements in Kashmir Valley sharpened their efforts at disrupting peace and public life through protests, bandhs, demonstrations and sporadic violent acts in Srinagar and other major towns, and in the countryside. For the first time, some of these organisations repeated old history taking advantage of a weak and dithering administrative machinery that watched helplessly as Hindus (Kashmiri Pandits) were made targets of hate. To start with, they chose soft targets of Hindu temples, spread across towns and villages of Kashmir, for destruction. In February 1986, in Anantnag district alone, twenty-two temples were burnt or partially burnt, and other adjoining structures damaged. Idols were desecrated and broken and temple property looted and temple land occupied. At one or two places the premises were converted into mosques. Similar destructive treatment was meted out to seven temples in Srinagar district, three temples in Budgam district, three temples in Kupwara district, and four temples in Baramula district (Raina, 2004:29-31).

Between 1987 and 1990 further such attacks were made, and serious damage was done to fifteen places of worship of Hindus. The Government of India in a statement in Indian Parliament on March 12, 1993, admitted that 38 places of worship had been damaged in Jammu and Kashmir State, 13 in 1989, 9 in 1990 and 16 in 1991. These destructive activities continued well beyond this period without any remedial action being taken by the state or central government at any level except for some empty promises (ibid 31-37).

But this was just the beginning; worse things were to follow. Soon the attacks were extended to private property and life and limb of individual Kashmiri Pandits. The first two three deaths were reported from Srinagar in 1987-1988. Then came the shocking assassination of Pt Tika Lal Taploo, prominent and widely popular advocate and BJP leader, on September 13, 1989 near his home at Habakadal, Srinagar. It was soon followed by the killing of Pt Nil Kant Ganju, retired session judge on November 4, 1989 at Hari Singh Street, Srinagar. Smt. Sheela Tikoo, a housewife, had been killed on November 1, 1989, while carrying a bag of vegetables near her home at Habakadal. Pt. Prem Nath Bhat, a senior advocate and a well-liked and well-known person was killed at Anantnag on December 27,1989. So the sporadic killings went on.

In the meantime, a dramatic incident took place on December 8, 1989. Dr. Rubaiya Sayeed, daughter of Mufti Mohd Sayeed, the then Home Minister of India, was reported to have been kidnapped in Srinagar by JKLF secessionists. They threatened to kill her unless 5 of their leading militant activists were released from police detention, unconditionally. At that time Farooq Abdullah was the Chief Minister of the state, and

V. P. Singh was the Prime Minister of India. After negotiations through intermediaries with the JKLF leaders the five militants were released by the government on December 13, 1989 followed by the release of Dr. Rubaiya Sayeed two hours later by the militants (Grover: 64- 65). This was a happy ending to a dramatic incident except for the fact that the authorities were obliged to compromise on the militants' terms. The government was shown as weak and vacillating while the militants were seen as dictating terms to it as a dominant force. The release of the top militants had a negatively cathartic effect on a section of the public mind in the Valley and led to euphoric reactions (no doubt misguided) when for three days and nights thousands of people in downtown Srinagar came on the streets in processions shouting slogans, bursting crackers and singing songs in favour of 'azadi' (freedom) (see Sidhva in Grover: 746-47). It may be noted here that JKLF is an outfit that seeks independence for Jammu and Kashmir. After some time the reality dawned on the people that 'azadi' was not round the corner and the concept was yet vague and illusory in terms of the geo-political realities of the situation. However, this particular incident gave a great psychological boost to the subversive and violent activities of the militants, the terrorists and the potential terrorists. It seems that at some higher levels of the terrorist outfits operating in Kashmir Valley there had been a policy decision to terrorise, kill, and drive away the Kashmiri Pandits from the Kashmir Valley in 1989-90 to transform it into a 100% Muslim area.

Sometime in the future the inside story will be known.

According to the information painstakingly collected and recorded by Panun Kashmir Movement, (Raina 2004: 77-94) during the year 1990 alone, 311 Kashmiri Pandits (including some women) were killed by the terrorists in Srinagar and other districts in the Valley. During the period and later, several hundred Hindu homes and shops etc. were also burnt, damaged and looted and building materials taken away.

It was under such unfortunate circumstances that the tragic mass exodus of the Kashmiri Pandits spread across the Kashmir Valley took place in 1989-90. They had to save their lives, the honour of their women and elders and the future of their children.

In January 1990, the state of Jammu and Kashmir was under the governor's rule and governor Jagmohan, sensitive to the plight of the Kashmiri Pandits fleeing from the Valley, announced a relief package at Jammu to reduce their misery and pain. This decision was timely and helped them survive and uplift their spirit to deal with an extremely adverse situation. Many Kashmiri Pandits came to Delhi and here also the same relief measures were extended to them. Many others with contacts and relations in other parts of India went to those places. Many Kashmiri Pandits, with some private resources, did not seek refuge in the relief camps at Jammu or Delhi etc. However, they accepted whatever relief they could claim while living outside the relief camps. Since 1990 more Kashmiri Pandits, out of the few thousands, which for some reason or the other chose or had to stay back, were killed at various places (we shall come to that later), and some more were obliged to abandon their homes in the Valley.

For the violence, destruction and terror unleashed by the Pakistan-inspired and Pakistan-aided terrorist organisations in the state against the Kashmiri Pandits, the reasons were political, as there have been no local causes or history of any serious hostility between them and the Kashmiri Muslims. The process of "ethnic cleansing" has obviously been aimed at weakening secular India's hold over the Kashmir Valley in particular. For a proud and progressive community, committed to the glory of their motherland, to become refugee in their own country, will rank among the greatest tragedies in the annals of free India. For the Kashmiri Pandits, history had repeated itself after six centuries but under circumstances least anticipated.

Research Project

All this happened fourteen years back. Towards the last quarter of the year 2002, when we launched this Research Project and conducted our basic survey around that time, the tragic event of the mass exodus of the Kashmiri Pandits from Kashmir Valley was about 12 years old. During 2001-2002 the Kashmir Education, Culture and Science Society (KECSS), New Delhi, had organised a few seminars and discussions, where speakers made repeated references to the EXODUS and its causes and implications etc. We had also observed that during all these years wherever Kashmiri Pandits met, in social gatherings or other meetings, there were constant references to this event and people expressed their personal opinions about all aspects of the matter. However, in 2001 we realised, more sharply than ever, the urgent need for a research based report on the 'migrant' Kashmiri Pandits to assess -

a) The economic, social, and cultural impact of the uprooting of the community on a mass scale during 1989-90.

b) The process of rehabilitation of the community in Jammu and Delhi where vast majority of the 'migrants' had settled down. Also to make a comparative check on the members of the community still living in The Kashmir Valley.

c) The problems especially faced by women and children before and after migration and their role in the entire process.

We looked around but could not lay our hands on any report of this kind, published or unpublished though we heard of some surveys having been done by some organisations. One such survey had been carried out by the All India Kashmiri Samaj, at Jammu in 1990-91. They had used a four-page questionnaire and covered 1956 households with a population of over 10,000. The data are lying in Delhi School of Economics, Delhi University, but no report is available yet.

However, in accordance with our above stated thoughts we made a proposal with a research design and budget estimates etc. in June 2001 and submitted it for approval to the Department of Women and Child Development, Ministry of Human Resources Development, Government of India. After a series of discussions at various levels in the Ministry, spread over several weeks and months we received the letter of approval and sanction of grants in May 2002. We were able to start our work on the Research Project, after the grants were released on September 12, 2002. By early 2003 major fieldwork had been done in Delhi, Jammu and the Kashmir Valley. Some 800 questionnaires were canvassed in the three regions of which, after screening, 743 were found valid for use in the project. This report has been written after tabulation of the quantitative data and collation of the qualitative data.

Research Methods and Techniques

The universe for our study is the population of Kashmiri Pandits that has migrated from the Valley, especially since 1989-90, and settled in Delhi and Jammu, as also those few families who have stayed back in their villages and towns, for one reason or the other or because of their optimistic belief that happier days will return.

No accurate figures of the total population of Kashmiri Pandits is available. Popular estimates vary from 500, 000 to 700,000. Of these three lakhs are believed to have left the Valley in 1989-90 itself. According to official records of Jammu and Kashmir government (as per statement of the revenue minister in the State Assembly on 03-04-2001) the following figures are available regarding migrant Kashmiri Pandits —

A. (a) Families registered with Relief Commissioners Jammu: 29565.
   (b) Migrant families registered in Delhi: 19339.
   (c) Migrant families registered in other Indian states: 1860.

   [a + b + c: Total population = 2,30,000 (approximately)]

B. Kashmiri Pandit families still living in the Valley (2001 figures): 1216 [Total population = 8000 (approximately)]

   Note: Jammu and Kashmir government information reproduced in "Naad" New Delhi, dated May 2003, page 3. The population figures have been marked out on the basis average family size, based on official information and our own data, which broadly tally.

It has been widely believed, as stated above, that around 300,000 Kashmiri Pandits left Kashmir Valley during the Exodus in 1989-90. Not all of them are registered as 'MIGRANTS' anywhere. As such the official figures regarding the registered families and their estimated population seem to be more or less correct.

Since the Jammu region and the state of Delhi have the largest concentration of migrant Kashmiri Pandits we decided to choose statistically valid samples from these places. Also, we decided to explore the possibility of covering a reasonable number (around 50) of households from Kashmir Valley for comparison and to serve as a control group. For our survey we selected households at random mostly from the relief camps/ localities and some from other areas in the following manner:

REGION	COVERAGE
Delhi (in different areas)	250 households (population 1277)
Jammu (Muthi, Purkhoo, Mishriwala, Nagrota, Udhampur Camps etc.)	340 households (population 1706)
Kashmir (Srinagar, Baramula, Pulwama, and Anantnag districts)	153 households (population 1017)

Total number = 743 households
Total population = 4000 people

The samples are statistically valid region-wise and overall and both in terms of the number of households and population covered. The coverage in Kashmir was extraordinarily good and much beyond our expectations. This was possible thanks to our very resourceful local coordinator Dr. Satyabhama Razdan and the cooperation of a number of young men and women (some of them University teachers and students).

The following methods were used for the collection of the required data:

1. SCHEDULE (Questionnaire):

A detailed schedule was printed to collect quantitative data on

a) Demography.
b) Literacy and education.
c) Employment and income.
d) Assets lost (on migration).
e) Assets acquired (post migration).
f) Health status.

2. INTERVIEW

Qualitative data were collected through interviews of informants and also family members, men and women about all aspects of their life before and after migration and their views about all matters of their concern. Each schedule had a few blank pages to record their statements most conveniently.

2. CASE STUDIES

Households and individuals with specially interesting experiences of relevance to our investigations were interviewed at greater length to gain deeper insight into their problems and issues at stake. We listened to and recorded their opinions and comments with great care.

3. LITERATURE CONSULTED

We have taken note of some of the published material on the history of Kashmir and politics and growth of militancy in the state for gaining a little more clarity in our own understanding of the complex situation prevailing there.

Finally, we would like to emphasise that this work is not meant to be some kind of an assessment of the militancy/terrorism in Kashmir. Nor do we pretend to have built any theories to prove or disprove anything. This study has attempted an objective look at the situation with empathy for all those who have suffered deep pain, and with shared joy for all those who have emerged into light, from darkness and gloom.

Chapter – 2

DEMOGRAPHIC PROFILE

The survey (2002-2003) covers a total of 743 households with a total population of 4000 individuals. Of these 2083 are males and 1917 are females (see Table I to V). The survey has been conducted in three major locations i.e. Delhi state, Jammu region and Kashmir Valley covering 250 households (population 1277), 340 households (population 1706) and 153 households (population 1017) respectively.

The universe for our study is specially constituted by the Kashmiri Pandit migrants who were uprooted on a mass scale from their homes and hearths in Kashmir Valley in 1990 as a result of severe hostility and violence and threats of violence, unleashed there for almost a year prior to this tragic event. But, in general terms our universe is also the entire Kashmiri Pandit community which, barring a few thousand, lives entirely outside Kashmir Valley. Members of the community have been leaving the Valley 1948 onwards in small numbers for studies and in search of jobs and livelihood. The community is now scattered in different parts of India, and many have gone to the USA, Europe, and other parts of the world. The current population of Kashmiri Pandits in India and elsewhere should be around half a million, though accurate figures are not available.

The population of 4000 covered under our study through random sampling mostly at migrant camps in Delhi and

Jammu and residential areas in Kashmir Valley (in Srinagar city and across the countryside) is a statistically valid sample. The analysis of this sample gives us useful data that indicate general trends in the demographic profile of the community.

The sex ratio (females per thousand males) in our sample is 920 with a range of974 (Delhi), 908 (Jammu) and 876 (Kashmir) (see Tables VIA & B).

Let us compare these figures with 2001 census figures for Kashmir Valley 914, Jammu and Kashmir State 900, and India 933. As is clear from the above figures, the sex ratio in Jammu and Kashmir State and Kashmir Valley is well below the national figure. Our sample supports this trend in terms of the average figures.

The demographic Tables I to IV show the distribution of the sample population, in actual figures and percentages, sex-wise in and across standard age grades (as used in the census) overall and region-wise.

The Tables make interesting reading. Eleven percent population is below 10 years and the segment below 20 years constitutes 25 percent of the sample population (see Table V also). In other words, about one-fourth of the population belongs to the 0-19 age group. But the largest single segment is the 20-39 age group ie., 38 percent This means that nearly two thirds (62%) of this population is below 40 years old. The 40-59 age group makes up for another 26% (one-fourth) of the sample population. The 60 plus group is equal to one-eighth (12%) segment and if we were to count the people of 50 years and above group they will be over 23% (about one fourth) of the population.

To sum up in simple round terms the picture we get is like this:

The segments of below 20 years and 50 years plus age groups together constitute about one half of the population

(48%). The segment of 20 to 49 years age groups makes up for the other half (52%).

The fertility level of a community is indicated by the ratio of children in the 0-6 age group to the total population (see Tables VI A and B). From the 2001 census we have gathered data on this subject for Kashmir Valley, Jammu and Kashmir state and India. The percentage of children in the 0-6 age group for each population is 15.8, 14.2 and 15.4 respectively. The percentage of female children in each case is below that of male children.

By comparison our sample population shows a much lower rate (less than half) at only 7.5% children in the 0-6 group in the sample population. The regional samples show some variation, the lowest percentage (6.5) is in Kashmir sample and the highest (8.6) in Delhi sample, the Jammu sample at 7.4% stands in the middle.

The very low index of fertility among the Kashmiri Pandits post-migration and even those still living in Kashmir Valley should not be a matter of surprise. Human fertility can be adversely affected by the kind of traumatic circumstances, which the community has had to face and grapple with prior to, during and after the mass migration in 1990. The loss of home and hearth, heavy material losses, destruction of community bonding and community life, cruelties inflicted on individual members, both men, women and children across the Valley, the verbal and physical insults and humiliations suffered, the sense of betrayal by friends and neighbours and the deep sense of insecurity nurtured over decades have left scars on the collective mind of the community. The psychological damage can have a negative inpact on all aspects of social life including childbearing activity. However, there have been many other contributory factors e.g. the arduous task of rebuilding life in unfamiliar places and unfavourable circumstances. The extreme heat and dust of Jammu and the Indian plains in contrast to the salubrious climate of Kashmir did severe damage to the health and morale of many individuals unused to living in such a climate and such weather conditions.

The living space and condition in the migrant camps have been absolutely inadequate and substandard. The Kashmiri families so used to living in spacious three storeyed houses had to move into flimsy shelters and one room tents with no space for toilet, cooking, or proper rest or privacy for men, women and children. Water was scarce in the scorching heat of the summer and the rain flooded the tents in the rainy season. And when the winds blew, strong and furious, many weather-beaten tents got torn and blown off leaving the inmates naked in spirit, mind, and body!

Over the years the conditions have improved somewhat. There are no tents any more; their place has been taken by one-room tenements. But toilets and kitchen spaces and privacy and proper maintenance are still lacking. Among the young men and women jobs are hard to come by even when they are suitably educated. Under these circumstances in many cases the need to delay, space, and even avoid having children might be a matter of cruel compulsion.

The average size of family/household (see Table VII) in our total sample works out to be 5.4 with a membership of 2.8 males and 2.6 females. However, in comparison with the Delhi and Jammu samples (5.1 and 5.0 average household membership) the average membership in the Kashmir sample is 6.6 that is an additional membership of one and half persons. The reason is that much of the data from Kashmir Valley covers the households in the countryside, which are still intact as small extended families and hence larger in size. On the other hand, the migrant families at Jammu and in Delhi have, after migration broken up and become smaller units as some members have moved out or away, for one reason or the other, under compulsion of the changed circumstances.

Table 1
Demographic Details

Grand Total (743 Households)						
Age Group	*Male*	%	*Female*	%	*Total*	%
0-4	106	5.09	83	4.33	189	4.73
5-9	124	5.95	127	6.62	251	6.28
10-14	139	6.67	118	6.16	257	6.43
15-19	144	6.91	150	7.82	294	7.35
20-24	176	8.45	169	8.82	345	8.63
25-29	204	9.79	222	11.58	426	10.65
30-34	214	10.27	200	10.43	414	1035
35-39	184	8.83	167	8.71	351	8.78
40-44	166	7.97	138	7.20	304	7.60
45-49	116	5.57	136	7.09	252	6.30
50-59	129	6.19	109	5.69	238	5.95
55-59	104	4.99	99	5.16	203	5.08
>60	277	13.30	199	10.38	476	11.90
TOTAL	2083	100%	1917	100%	4000	100%

Table II
Demographic Details

Delhi (250 Households)						
Age Group	*Male*	%	*Female*	%	*Total*	%
0-4	42	6.49	30	4.76	72	5.64
5-9	39	6.03	51	8.10	90	7.05
10-14	32	4.95	39	6.19	71	5.56
15-19	41	6.34	44	6.98	85	6.66
20-24	41	6.34	36	5.71	77	**6.03**
25-29	66	10.20	61	9.68	127	9.95
30-34	78	12.06	81	12.86	159	12.45
35-39	61	9.43	56	8.89	117	9.16
40-44	53	8.19	41	651	94	7.36
45-49	36	5.56	43	6.83	79	6.19
50-59	31	4.79	29	4.60	60	4.70
55-59	37	5.72	35	5.56	72	5.64
>60	90	13.91	84	1333	174	13.63
Total	647	100%	630	100%	1277	100%

Table III
Demographic Details

Jammu (340 Households)

Age Groups	*Male*	%	*Female*	%	*Total*	%
0-4	41	4.59	29	3.57	70	4.10
5-9	63	7.05	56	6.90	119	6.98
10-14	81	9.06	59	7.27	140	8.21
15-19	69	7.72	76	9.36	145	8.50
20-24	83	9.28	78	9.61	161	9.44
25-29	84	9.40	93	11.45	177	10.38
30-34	83	9.28	81	9.98	164	9.61
35-39	85	9.51	79	9.73	164	9.61
40-44	75	8.39	57	7.02	132	7.74
45-49	41	4.59	53	6.53	94	5.55
50-59	48	5.37	44	5.42	92	3.91
55-59	34	3.80	36	4.43	70	4.10
>60	107	11.97	71	8.74	178	10.43
Total	894	100%	812	100%	1706	100%

Table IV
Demographic Details

Kashmir (153 Households)						
Age Group	*Male*	%	*Female*	%	*Total*	%
0-4	23	4.24	24	5.05	47	4.62
5-9	22	4.06	20	4.21	42	4.13
10-14	26	4.80	20	4.21	46	4.52
15-19	34	6.27	30	6.32	64	6.29
20-24	52	9.59	55	11.58	107	10.52
25-29	54	9.96	68	14.32	122	12.00
30-34	53	9.78	38	8.00	91	8.95
35-39	38	7.01	32	6.74	70	6.88
40-44	38	7.01	40	8.42	78	7.67
45-49	39	7.20	40	8.42	79	7.77
50-59	50	9.23	36	7.58	86	8.46
55-59	33	6.09	28	5.89	61	6.00
>60	80	14.76	44	9.26	124	12.19
Total	542	100%	475	100%	1017	100%

Table V
Age Grades: As Percentages

Age Groups	*Delhi*	*Jammu*	*Kashmir*	*Total*
0-19	25%	28%	20%	24%
20-39	37%	39%	38%	38%
40-59	24%	23%	30%	26%
60+	14%	10%	12%	12%
	100	100	100	100

Table VI'A'

Population and Sex Ratio (census data)

Population and Sex Ratio			*Children In 0-6 Years Age Group*					
SOURCE; Census of India 2001 provisional population totals/Paper 1,2001, suppl.		*Females per 1000 males*	*Population (Children 0-6 Age group)*			*As Percentage of Total Population*		
Universe	Total Population	Sex Ratio	Persons	Male	Female	Persons	Male	Female
India	1,027,015,247	933	157,845,618	81,890,147	75,955,147	15.4	8.0	7.4
Jammu & Kashmir	1,0069917	900	1,431,182	7,38,839	6,92,343	14.2	7.3	6.9
Kashmir Valley	54,41,341	914	7,48,692	3,77,466	3,71,226	15.8	7.0	6.8

Table VI 'B'

Kashmiri Pandits : Project Data

(A) Delhi Sample	1277	974	110	57	53	8.6	4.5	4.1
(B) Jammu Sample	1706	908	127	71	56	7.4	4.1	3.3
(C) Kashmir Sample	1017	876	66	34	32	6.5	3.3	3.2
Total	4000	920	303	162	131	7.5	4.0	3.5

Chapter – 3

LITERACY AND EDUCATION

The Kashmiri Pandits, like the Brahmins all over the country, have over the millennia been intellectual elites, deeply committed to the pursuit of knowledge and learning. Their concerns were aesthetics and philosophical and spiritual thought processes as they relate to and affect human destiny. Reaching the highest levels of scholarship as also spiritual attainment they commanded great respect in Kashmiri society. It was through such sustained endeavours and devotion to learning with a large spiritual content, that Kashmiri Pandits earned for Kashmir the worldwide reputation as a great seat of Sanskrit and Buddhist learning. All this happened in the pre-Islamic phase of Kashmir's history.

The Brahmins in Kashmir as elsewhere in India, also pursued knowledge to work as teachers and administrators - advisors, astrologers and astronomers, medical practitioners, interpreters of religious texts and epics for the common people and of course guides and supervisors of religious rituals and ceremonies in day to day life of the members of the Kashmiri society. But in the process of their preoccupation with knowledge and learning the Brahmins in Kashmir (and India) have been averse to non-intellectual occupations involving manual labour and the trades of the artisans for earning their bread and butter *(hakh bata).*

However, under the changing circumstances following Muslim rule and the annexation of Kashmir by the Mughal emperor, Akbar, Kashmiri Pandits also took to studying Persian, and at later stages Urdu and English besides Sanskrit and Hindi. This enabled them to take up office jobs, at almost all levels in the hierarchy of the local bureaucracy and provide vital and accessible link in the interface between the general public (Muslims, Hindus and the rest) with the government and political authorities at the higher levels. Since the Kashmiri Muslims had been educationally backward till about the sixties of the last century, Kashmiri Pandits had played an important role in this area even at the height of the social and political prejudice and the dominance of the Muslim rule in Kashmir. However, 1947 onwards the process of squeezing them out of this space started, and continued. The Kashmiri Pandits were also the first community in Kashmir to study English language and literature and modern science and technology within the available facilities during the Maharaja's rule in Kashmir and the British rule in India. This policy is being followed to this day in fact, with even greater vigour and enthusiasm by boys and girls, men and women because that is the ticket to employment all over India and even outside the country (the USA and European countries etc.). Also, one could reach out and touch positions of high merit and excellence anywhere in the world. The relative neglect of Sanskrit learning in Kashmir (and elsewhere in India) is directly related to the 200 years of British rule in India and the functioning of the economies and the job markets within the country and around the world during the last century.

The above description is purely parenthetical to the discussion of our project data on the literacy and educational level of the Kashmiri Pandit migrants in Delhi and Jammu and those still living in Kashmir at the time of this survey. The point of note is to observe the historical context of the deep concern for education among the Kashmiri Pandits especially while they are struggling against all odds as an uprooted community to re-establish itself, to renew its vitality and energise its vision with an optimistic outlook.

Literacy

The extent and rates of literacy among men and women in a community is one of the most important criteria for judging its potential and capacity for self-development in all areas of day-to-day living. Literacy means access to relevant knowledge outside the routine areas of social/cultural interaction and oral traditions. It grants an individual a high degree of autonomy for accessing knowledge of one's own choice and interest for extending areas of one's awareness.

To get a detailed picture of the literacy and educational levels of the Kashmiri Pandits in our survey frame let us study the Tables I (A & B) II III and IV. The overall literacy rate for our sample is 89.15% (Table I A) and for men only it works out to be about 97%, while for women it is about 81%. That means against 3% illiteracy among men it is 19% among women. This can be attributed to lack of proper and convenient facilities for women in the rural areas, especially those of the older generation. Also, this is due to relative neglect and indifference at the social level of women's education. So on the slightest excuse girls were discouraged from joining schools or going for higher classes to a school further away from their village homes. In fact the women's education among the Kashmiri Pandits received a setback during the prolonged Muslim rule in Kashmir for various social and political reasons. However, in their new places the migrant families are making optimum use of the locally available facilities for both boys and girls.

The above survey was conducted towards the close of the year 2002 and early 2003. Comparing this data with the 2001 census figures, we find that the overall literacy rate for Jammu and Kashmir is 54.46, and about 66% and 42% for males and females, respectively. For India as a whole the literacy rates are 65.4% (for all) and about 76% and 54% for males and females respectively. Obviously, our Kashmiri Pandit sample of 3697 people is at a much higher literacy level than both Jammu and Kashmir state, and India as a whole. A good sign, but not unexpected. We expect that in the coming decade (maybe by the next census) Kashmiri Pandits as a community will be 100% literate. (It may be noted here that for computation of the literacy rates, children 0-6 age group are excluded by the census department and here also we have followed the same procedure).

The highest rate of literacy, nearly 100% is shown by the male population in our Delhi group and same for women at about 91%. The lowest literacy rate for the males is in our Kashmir sample (92.32%) and for the females the lowest rate of about 75% belongs to our Jammu sample.

As we have observed in our other chapters (2, 4, 5, 6) of this study, our Delhi group is the leader in all respects e.g. better male/female ratio, employment and income levels, (both among men and women) educational attainments, and faster pace of recovery, etc. This has got to do with their background (towns and progressive rural areas) and the better economic and social opportunity in a mega city like Delhi. The capital city has helped them breathe in freedom and discard the negative baggage of mindless "minoritysm" and the destructive discrimination that the community has suffered from, for half a century. By comparison, the Jammu based migrants and the

Kashmir Valley residents have a lot of catching up to do. We *may* add here that the Delhi figures are better also because 16.8% of our sample households have migrated to Delhi prior to 1989 and they are better established here.

A. EDUCATION: GENERAL

The highest of educational **levels** and qualitative achievements reached by people in our sample can be summed up as under (see Tables II, III, IV and V).

1) The general Table (II) shows that overall -

   a) 21.2% are graduates in arts, commerce, education etc (over 1/5 of the sample)

   b) 11% (over 1/10 of sample) hold degrees in science, engineering and medicines etc. and 4% members (1/25 of sample) have got masters' degrees in arts, commerce, and education etc.

   c) 21.6% members (over 1/5 of sample) have done high school and 16.6% (1/6 of sample) have cleared the senior secondary school (class 12) examination in arts/sciences.

   d) The male/female ratio in literacy and education is 56.5/43.5

The total picture is quite good and on way to further improvement as more and more children are attending schools in their new settlements.

2) Tables III and IV throw further light on the educational pattern of our samples in Delhi, Jammu and Kashmir.

I. Delhi

   a) Has the highest literacy rate and highest achievements in education.

b) Among the males 20% have degrees in science, engineering or medicine etc. (1/5 of sample).

   And 28% have graduated in arts, commerce, and education etc.

c) Over 1/5 males (21%) have passed class 12 and about 1/10 (9.7%) class 10 school examinations.

d) Among women nearly 1/3 (30.50) have degrees in arts, commerce, and education. Nearly 20% have passed class 12 and 16% class 10 examinations. Also 8% have degrees in science, engineering, and medicine etc.

e) In Delhi there are also 15 M. Sc. (8+7) and 3 Ph. D. (2+1) degree holders.

II. Jammu

a) In this group there are 16 M.Sc. (13+3) 11% graduates in science, engineering or medicine and 17.4% are degree holders in arts, commerce and education. 26% males have passed their high school and 15% their class 12 examination.

b) Among the females nearly 1/3 have passed their class 10 (32.4%), 16.6% are graduates in arts/commerce and education and 6.7% have degrees in technical courses.

III. Kashmir

a) Here we have among the males 17% arts/commerce and education graduates and 11.7% science and engineering or medical degree holders. Nearly 1/5 males have done their class 10 course.

b) The. females show comparable achievements, about ¼ are matriculates, 13% have passed class 12, 17.6% are arts/commerce graduates and about 6% have degrees in science/engineering or medicine. There are 3 M. Sc. and 5 M.A. degree holders among them.

B. EDUCATION: PROFESSIONAL

In a total population of 3296 educated people 383 (11.6%) have qualified in specialised professional courses. Out of these 255 are men (7.7%) and 128 are women (3.9%). A big chunk of those (39%) are qualified teachers with postgraduate degrees in education and some have done diplomas in education. The next big group (36%) is that of people with degrees in engineering, computer science, information technology etc. Add to that another 8.8% diploma holders. The medical field is poorly represented with only 4.4% degree holders (14 men plus 3 women). With the addition of 2.8 percent diploma holders it still amounts to only 7.2%.

An area-wise appraisal proves, once again, the leadership of the Delhi group in higher professional categories. It has 69 (53%) men and 20 (30%) women engineers etc., 8 male doctors and 1 female doctor. Next comes Jammu with 29 male (37%) 1.2 female engineers etc (26%). Kashmir has 9 male engineers and 1 female engineer. Jammu has 3 plus 2 doctors and Kashmir only 3 male doctors. Teachers make a big crowd everywhere. Delhi has 12+2 MBA degree holders, Jammu 3, and Kashmir none.

The distribution of professionally qualified people is like this:

Total		Males	Females
Delhi	198	131	67
	(51.7%)	(51.4%)	(52.3%)
Jammu	125	79	49

Total		Males	Females
	(32.6%)	(31.0%)	(38.3%)
Kashmir	60	45	15
	(15.7%)	(17.6%)	(10.4%)

It is worth noting that more than half (above 51%) the professional people, both among men and women, belong to Delhi group. The other group (below 50%) of professionals are shared by Jammu and Kashmir. Kashmir has the least number (10.4%) of women professionals against 38% in Jammu and 52% in Delhi.

In conclusion we can say that for the Kashmiri Pandits, their greatest strength in good times and bad, has been their higher levels of education and literacy (must be one of the highest among the Indian communities). This combined with their sense of pride, resilience and capacity for adjustment under difficult circumstances makes them a community of eternal survivors.

Educating their children remains their top priority under all conditions. All kinds of sacrifices can be made with this objective in view. We have heard some true stories of some mothers of migrant children having accompanied their sons and daughters, going to join distant colleges in other parts of India, and having stayed there for prolonged periods in rented rooms to help them get home food and boost their morale. May god bless them all!

Table I'A'
Literacy

	Population (0-6 age group excluded)			*Literature*			*Literacy Rates*		
Region	*Persons*	*Males*	*Females*	*Persons*	*Males*	*Females*	*Persons*	*Males*	*Females*
Delhi	1167	590	577	1113	589	524	9537%	99.83%	90.81%
Jammu	1579	823	756	1368	803	565	86.63%	97.56%	74.73%
Kashmir	951	508	443	815	469	346	85.70%	92.32%	78.10%
Grand Total	3697	.1921	1776	3296	1861	1435	89.15%	96.87%	81.80%

(Research project survey data, 2002-2003)

Table I'B'

	Literacy Rate		
	Persons	*Males.*	*Females*
Jammu & Kashmir	54.46%	65.75%	41.82%
India	65.37%	75.85%	54.16%

(Source: Census of India, 2001)

Table II
Literacy and Education: Total

Region	*Delhi*		*Jammu*		*Kashmir*		*Total*			
Level	M	F	M	F	M	F	M	F	M+F	%
Literate	14	17	25	20	10	20	49	57	106	3.2
Class V	23	37	52	51	25	31	100	119	219	6.6
Class VIII	29	42	110	83	50	55	189	180	369	11.2
Class X	57	83	210	183	93	85	360	351	711	21.6
Class XII	125	103	122	76	75	45	322	224	546	16.6
Pre-degree and diploma course	18	5	15	6	42	20	75	31	106	3.2
BA, B. Com, B. Ed., etc.	165	160	140	94	80	61	385	315	700	21.2
MA, M. Com, M.Ed, MBA Etc.	31	27	28	11	31	5	90	43	133	4.0
B.Sc., Technical, and Medical degree	117	42	88	38	55	20	260	100	360	11.0

MSc.	8	7	13	3	8	3	29	13	42	13
Ph.D.	2	1	-	-	-	1	2	2	4	0.1
Total	589	524	803	565	469	346	1861	1435	3296	100

Table III

Literacy and Education: Delhi

Level	*M*	%	*F*	%	*Total*	%
Literate	14	2.4	17	3.2	31	2.8
Class V	23	3.9	37	7.0	60	5.4
Class VIII	29	4.9	42	8.0	71	6.4
Class X	57	9.7	83	15.8	140	12.6
Class XII	125	21.2	103	19.6	228	20.5
Pre-degree and diploma course	18	3.0	5	0.9	23	2.0
BA, B. Com, B. Ed. etc.	165	28.0	160	30.5	325	29.2
MA, M. Com, MEd., MBA Etc.	31	5.3	27	5.1	58	5.2
B. Sc., Technical and Medical degree	117	19.9	42	8.0	15.9	14.3
M. Sc.	8	1.3	7	1.3	15	1.3
Ph.D.	2	0.3	1	0.2	3	0.3
Total	589	100	524	100	1113	100

Table IV
Literacy and Education: Jammu & Kashmir

Region	*Jammu*						*Kashmir*					
Level	*Males*	%	*Females*	%	*Total*	%	*Males*	%	*Females*	%	*Total*	%
Literate	25	3.1	20	3.5	45	3.3	10	2.1	20	5.8	30	3.7
Class V	52	6.5	51	9.0	103	7.5	25	5.3	31	8.9	56	6.9
Class VIII	110	13.7	83	14.7	193	14.1	50	10.7	55	15.9	105	12.9
Class X	210	26.1	183	32.4	393	28.7	93	19.8	85	24.6	178	21.8
Class XII	122	15.2	76	13.4	198	14.5	75	16.0	45	13.0	120	14.7
Pre-degree and diploma course	15	1.8	6	1.0	21	1.5	42	8.9	20	5.8	62	7.6
BA, B. Com, B. Ed. etc.	140	17.4	94	16.6	234	17.1	80	17.0	61	17.6	141	17.3
MA, M. Com, M.Ed., MBA Etc.	28	3.5	11	2.0	39	2.8	31	6.6	5	1.4	36	4.4
B.Sc., Technical and medical degree	88	11.0	38	6.7	126	9.2	55	11.7	20	5.8	75	9.2
M. Sc.	13	1.6	3	0.5	16	1.2	8	1.7	3	0.9	11	1.3
Ph.D.	-	-	-	-	-	-	-	-	1	0.3	1	0.1
Total	802	100	565	100	1368	100	469	100	346	100	815	100

Table V
Education: Professional

Region				*Delhi*				*Jammu*				*Kashmir*						*Total*
Course	*M*	%	*F*	%	*M*	%	*F*	%	*M*	%	*F*	%	*M*	%	*F*	%	*M + F Total*	% *M + F*
BE. B. TECH.. M TECH.. BCA. MCA. 1. T. ETC	69	52.7	20	29.8	29	36.7	12	26.0	9	20.0	1	6.6	107	42.0	33	25.8	140	36.5
Medical degrees MBBS. MD. MS. BDS, BVS. BUMS ETC.	8	6.1	1	1.5	3	3.8	2	4.3	3	6.7	-	-	14	5.5	3	2.3	17	4.4
Diploma in Medicine/ Nursing	3	2.3	4	6.0	7	8.9	5	10.9	6	13.3	-	-	25	9.8	9	7.0	34	8.8
B Ed., M. Ed., Diploma in Education	21 (13+1+7)	16.0	35 (32+0+3)	52.2	33 (27+1+5)	41.8	23 (18+1+4)	50.0	25 (20+0+5)	55.5	12 (10+2+0)	80.0	79	31.0	70	54.7	149	39
MBA/ BBA	12	9.1	2	3.0	3	3.8	-	-	-	-	-	-	11	4.3	2	1.6	13	3.4
Miscellaneous subjects	6	4.6	1	1.5	3	3.8	2	4.3	2	4.4	1	6.6	15	5.9	4	3.1	19	5.0
Total	131	100	67	100	79	100	46	100	45	100	15	100	255	100	128	100	383	100
Percentage	66.2%		33.8%		63.2%		36.8%		75%		25%		66.6%		33.4 %			
Grand Total				198				125				60						383

Chapter – 4

EMPLOYMENT PATTERN

The employment situation among the uprooted Kashmiri Pandits now settled in Delhi and Jammu regions, and also those still living in Kashmir Valley, is graphically depicted (in terms of our research sample) in the Tables I (A), II, III, IV, V and Table VI.

The broad picture is as follows. In a population of 4000 surveyed under this study, only 1135 (28%) are earning money as monthly wages, mostly as government employees or as employees in private establishments or as petty shopkeepers. Only a small number is working on professional technical jobs with better salaries.

The region-wise percentage of the employed in our sample is 33% in Delhi, 22% in Jammu, and 34% in Kashmir. This averages at 28% for the entire sample. But in all the regions there is a strong bias in favour of males in employment (see Tables I to V). In Delhi against 52% males being employed less than 13% females are working. In Jammu against 37.5% working males only 5% females go out to work. So also in Kashmir, only 13% women work as compared to 52% men. In the total average only 9.5% women are earning wages outside their homes against 46% men.

The above employment levels in the three regions (Table I 'A') also show the earner-dependent ratio. For the entire sample it is 3 5 (that is each earner has to support 3.5 persons). The region-wise picture is 3.0 for Delhi, 3.0 for Kashmir, and 4.5 for Jammu. The employment levels in Delhi and Kashmir are nearly at par at 52% for men and around 13% for women. But for Jammu the situation is less bright, even for men at only 37.5% employment rate with a very poor 5% for women. The employment picture in the Jammu region is indeed very bad.

Jammu and Kashmir is an industrially backward state. Hence the job opportunities outside the public sector (government being the biggest employer) are very limited. And in the public sector there has been great discrimination against employing Kashmiri Pandits since 1948 both in Kashmir Valley and in Jammu region. After the mass exodus the situation has become worse. The Kashmiri Pandit migrants in the Jammu region are technically treated as residents of Kashmir Valley and are only eligible to apply for the government jobs in the Kashmir Valley quota and not in the Jammu quota. But since they are unable to apply and compete for jobs in Kashmir Valley, and being treated as not eligible for jobs in the Jammu region they remain losers all the way.

The situation in Kashmir Valley is different as many Kashmiri Pandits who have stayed back there beyond 1990 (the year of the mass exodus) are posted there as government employees (see Table VI) for specific duties. A look at the above Table shows that out of the 406 wage-earning persons in Kashmir 224 (65%) are the state and central government employees. In Delhi, the situation is comparatively better; it is a metropolis with many job opportunities outside the government. Besides, there is no pointed discrimination against the Kashmiri Pandit applicants or for that matter against any other community. Delhi, the capital of India is a place where hundreds of thousands of people from all over the country have settled down permanently of their own choice during the last half-a-century.

Let us once again scan the Tables II to VI to observe the kind of jobs held by the Kashmiri Pandits - men and women - in our sample overall and region-wise. The overall picture (Table II) among the men 44% serve in the government departments and about 9% are teachers (many in the government schools). For about 110 members the main source of income is relief (received every month in cash and kind as per the size of the family and the rules governing relief). Over 40% are holding private jobs or doing some private business on their own.

Though women hold 16% of the total jobs available they follow the same general pattern of employment as that of men. While 31% hold private jobs or do some private business, 35% serve the government, another 25% are teachers (in both government and private schools).

Region-wise, the broad picture is similar in Jammu region and Kashmir Valley, the scenario in Delhi is noticeably at variance with it. This is for reasons stated above. Let us look at the figures. About 73% men are working in the private sector i.e. private jobs (54%) or their own business (19%). Only 22% are doing government services and just 2% are teachers. Less than 1% rely mainly on government relief but more than 16% draw government pension post-retirement. Even among the women over 52% are in private jobs, doing private business or are business executives. While 26% are in government jobs 20% are teachers.

In the current situation and in real terms the most important section among women seriously seeking satisfactory and regular employment would be in the age grades 20-24, 25-29, and 30-34. Their total number in our sample is 591 (31% of female population). They are all educated and eager to work and assert their individuality and potential for positive contribution to the welfare of their families and their community in particular and society in general. We have talked to many of them during our fieldwork and we have been impressed with their sensitivity and sharpened awareness about their potential role in the changed environment and the need for constructive action at all levels by all concerned.

INCOME LEVELS

Now whatever be the nature and degree of employment among the members of the uprooted and disturbed community of Kashmiri Pandits, it is useful to get an idea about the kind of incomes they are able to generate in their jobs (see Table VIII). The Table shows a range of seven monthly income levels from below Rs. 2000/- to above Rs. 25000/- from the available data from our sample. As shown in Table VII the highest number of individuals are in the income brackets of Rs. 2000/- to Rs. 5000/- per month (578) and Rs. 5001/- to Rs. 10000/- (419) only 9 persons are in the Rs. 20000/- and above income group. All of them live in Delhi and are old migrants (pre-1990 and post-1947 category). So they are an exception to the general situation prevailing among the post-1990 migrant group. For a community that has suffered heavy economic losses and destruction of their immovable and movable property (homes and shops, household goods, commercial stocks, domestic cattle and trees, plantations and agricultural land etc.) high rate of unemployment or low-grade employment is not quite the answer.

The days of struggle continue even 12 years after the mass exodus. But visible efforts are being made by the community, in spite of the difficulties, to improve the situation in the coming decade with a lot of investment in the education of the younger generation in job oriented courses. This is the top priority with all individuals and households. "Education has been our mainstay," said a KP migrant lady "otherwise we would be starving or begging on the streets".

In a migrant camp at Jammu, a small group of young educated men told us that post-migration (in 12 years) not a single young man or young woman had been able to get a government job in their camp. Some of the youth have become directionless for want of a useful and profitable preoccupation. In our sample, 148 persons have only pension as their source of sustenance and for 110 persons government relief is the mainstay of their existence. Well, pension is a "fading income" and surviving solely on relief for prolonged periods cannot be a soul uplifting experience for young minds. They certainly look for better options in life. Should they not?

Table I 'A'
Employment Level

	Male			*Female*			*Total*			*Earner/ Dependent Ratio*
Region	*Population*	*No. of Employed*	*Percent-age*	*Population*	*No. of Em-ployed*	*Percent-age*	*Population M + F*	*No. of Employed*	*Percentage*	
Delhi	647	336	52.00 %	630	80	12.70 %	1277	416	32.60 %	3.0
Jammu	894	335	37.50 %	812	40	5.00 %	1706	375	22.00 %	4.5
Kashmir	542	282	52.00 %	475	62	13.00 %	1017	344	33.80 %	3.0
Grand Total	2083	953	45.70 %	1917	182	9.50%	4000	1135	28.40 %	3.5

Table I
Employment Pattern: Total

Regions	*Jammu*	*Delhi*	*Kashmir*	*Total*	*Percentage*
No. of Households	340	250	153	743	
Population	1706	1277	1017	4000	
Job Description	No. of Employees	No. of Employees	No. of Employees	No. of Employees	
Government Job	199	95	191	485	42.73
Medical Profession	5	2	7	14	1.23
Engineer Technical Job	2	2	5	9	0.80
Teacher	45	23	60	128	11.27
Private Job	48	212	14	274	24.14
Private Business	60	68	29	157	13.82
Business Executive	0	8	1	9	0.80
Daily Wage	6	0	0	6	0.53
Animal Husbandry/ Farming	6	0	15	21	1.85
Any Other	0	6	20	26	2.30
Not Mentioned	4	0	2	6	0.53
Total Employed	375	416	344	1135	100
Percentage	22 %	33%	34%	28%	

Table II
Employment Details: Total

Total Population: 4000 (2083 M +1917 F)						
Employment	*Male*	*%*	*Female*	*%*	*Total*	*%*
Government job	422	44.28	63	34.61	485	42.7
Medical profession	11	1.15	3	1.65	14	1.2
Engineer technical Job	8	0.84	1	0.55	9	0.8
Teacher	83	8.70	45	24.72	128	11.3
Private Job	230	24.13	44	24.17	274	24.1
Private Business	146	15.32	11	6.04	157	13.8
Business Executive	7	0.73	2	1.10	9	0.8
Daily wage	4	0.42	2	1.10	6	0.5
Animal husbandry/ Farming	19	2.00	2	1.10	21	1.8
Any Other	19	2.00	7	3.85	26	2.3
Not Mentioned	4	0.42	2	1.10	6	0.5
Not applicable	1130	39.44	1735	60.58	2865	100.00
Total	953	84.00	182	16.00	1135	100.00

Table V
Employment Details: Kashmir
Total Population: 1017 (542 M + 475 F)

Employment	*Male*	*Female*	*Total*
Government job	161	30	191
Medical profession	6	1	7
Engineer technical job	5	-	5
Teacher	43	17	60
Private job	11	3	14
Private Business	27	2	29
Business Executive	1	-	1
Daily wage	-	-	-
Animal husbandry/ Farming	13	2	15
Any other	14	6	20
Not Mentioned	1	1	2
Total Employed	228	62	344
Percentage	82.00	18.00	100

Table VI
Income Details

Sl. no.	*Income Level*	*Jammu*		*Delhi*		*Kashmir*		*Total*	
		Persons	*Percentage*	*Persons*	*Percentage*	*Persons*	*Percentage*	*Persons*	*Percentage*
1	Below Rs. 2000/-	55	322%	7	0.55%	67	6.59%	129	3.23 %
2	Rs. 2000/- to Rs. 5000/-	295	17.29 %	119	9.32 %	164	16.13 %	578	14.45 %
3	Rs. 5001 to Rs. 10000/-	141	8.26%	155	12.14%	123	12.09%	419	10.48%
4	Rs. 10001/-to Rs. 15,000/-	15	0.88 %	24	1.88%	24	236%	63	1.58%
5	Rs. 15,000/- to Rs. 20,000/-	7	0.41%	12	0.94%	3	029%	22	0.55%
6	Rs. 20,001/- to Rs. 25,000/-	Nil	Nil	1	0.08%	Nil	Nil	1	0.03 %
7	Above Rs. 25,000/-	Nil	Nil	8	0.63%	Nil	Nil	8	020%
8	Not Mentioned	20	1.17%	151	11.82%	12	1.18%	183	4.58 %
9	Not Applicable	1173	68.76%	800	62.65 %	624	6136%	2597	64.93%
	Total	1706	100 %	1277	100%	1017	100%	4000	100%

CHAPTER – 5

STATE OF HEALTH

The study of health status of a community is a very specialized area of social research and collection, and analyses of data need standard techniques and methodology for statistical validity and comparability. But it has not been possible to do so in this project as the main focus of our inquiry has been elsewhere. However, the kind of data we have been able to generate has served our purpose of gathering general trends in the health consciousness and health status of the community especially with reference to their women and children - more than a decade after their exit from the Valley.

In the section on health in our schedule (questionnaire) we had asked two kinds of questions from our informants: (a) regarding the particulars of family members who had died since 1990 (the year of mass exodus) and the cause of their death; and (b) regarding any serious health problems of surviving family members. The response to these questions has been fairly good and the data thus collected are presented in Tables I to II. Let us discuss the data on death and disease separately.

A. DEATH

The data on this topic were collected from all the three regions: Delhi, Jammu, and Kashmir. The Kashmir data is there for comparison though the sample households there do not constitute as migrants. We shall analyse the data region wise.

(a) DELHI (see Table I)

The total number of deaths reported during the period under reference (1990-2001) was 112 of which 69 (61.6%) were males and 43 (38.4%) were females. The major causes of death have been "depression" (34.0%), cardiac diseases (23.0%), brain haemorrhage/paralysis (10.7%) and cancer (9.0%). Together they account for more than three fourths (76.7%) of deaths. The remaining one-fourth share of deaths has been taken care of by diseases like diabetes (6.2%) sunstroke (5.3%) and "miscellaneous" and "natural" (unspecified) health problems (11.6%).

A close look at Table I shows that appreciably lesser number of women has suffered from some of the killer diseases mentioned above especially cancer, brain haemorrhage/ paralysis, diabetes and "miscellaneous" ailments. This is indicative of a better survival capacity among the women in the community. Also that their health care does not suffer from any neglect by comparison with the male members.

Another noteworthy thing is that not a single death has been reported in the 0-14 age group. One can safely conclude that the children's health remains a major concern of the community even in difficult times.

The death graph rises slowly from lower to higher age grades i.e. 7% in 15-44 age grade and 17% in 45-59 age group and then registers a sharp rise (76%) in the 60 plus age group. This is the stage when diseases having taken root earlier attain grave and chronic proportions and medical care becomes more expensive. Here the migrant community has faced serious difficulty in absence of any special medical assistance from the government agencies in the migrant camps at Jammu, Delhi and elsewhere. Such special assistance ought to have been a part of the general relief package extended to the beleaguered community in their camps and elsewhere.

(b) JAMMU (see Table II)

The deaths reported in our Jammu samples are almost evenly divided between males (51.5%) and females (48.5%). This may perhaps indicate that women's health has suffered some degree of neglect after migration to Jammu. In contrast the figures for Delhi and Kashmir are closely matching i.e., the ratio of male deaths to female deaths is approximately 3:2 in both places.

In Jammu group in 23% cases the specific cause of death could not be ascertained and another 15% deaths had occurred due to a variety of causes. Apart from these the major killers have been cardiac disease (12.5%), diabetes (11.8%), cancer (8.0%), depression (8.0%) and sunstroke (7.3%).

Further, more men than women have fallen victims to diseases like cancer, kidney failure, bronchitis, sunstroke etc. On the other hand more women than men have been killed by diseases like diabetes, cardiac problems, and miscellaneous ailments.

Here again by far the largest number of casualties belong to the 60 plus age group (64.0%). The rate declines sharply as we go down the age grade ladder i.e. 18.4% deaths in 45-59 group, 14.7% in the 15-44 age group and a meagre 3.0% in 0-14 age group. The four deaths reported in the last category have occurred due to accidents and not because of any disease.

(c) KASHMIR (see Table III)

Here the total number of deaths reported is 76 of which 47 (61.8%) are males and 29 (38.2%) are females. In this lot 24 deaths (31.6%) have been attributed to "natural causes" which means the diseases have not been named or identified in these cases. Otherwise, the biggest killer has been cancer (20% cases) followed by bronchitis (12%) gastric (9.2%) and cardiac (8.0%) problems. Men exhibit much more proneness to fatal diseases like cancer, cardiac problems, and natural (unidentified diseases) causes, whereas more women have succumbed to gastric ailments.

In our Kashmir sample also the same pattern with respect to age-related deaths is visible as in the case with our Delhi and Jammu samples. This reads as follows: 72.4% deaths in the 60 plus age group and a sharp downward trend as we descend the age grade scale i.e. 14.5% in 45-59 age group, 13.1% in 15-44 age group and no death reported in the 0-14 age group. This is the general picture with respect to all the three regional samples without very significant variation anywhere. This position seems to be supported by working out the ratio of deaths to the surviving population region wise (Table IV) which shows only slight variation.

(Table IV)
Population: Death Ratio

Region	*Sample Population*	*No. of Deaths (1990-2002)*	*Percentage*
Delhi	1277	112	8.8%
Jammu	1706	136	8.0%
Kashmir	1017	76	7.5%
Total	**4000**	**324**	8.1%

B. DISEASE

In section 'A' of this chapter we had a look at the data on the number of persons (age-wise and sex-wise) who had died between 1990 (the year of mass exodus from the Valley) and 2002 (the year when field work for this research project was conducted). We also looked into the cause of death of each person to know the kind of diseases that had proved fatal for the victims. These data were collected in all the three regions i.e., Delhi, Jammu and Kashmir. This has been one useful way of getting some idea about the state of health of the community in each of these places and for comparing the information gathered.

In this section we propose to have another look at this matter by analysing the data available regarding the prevalence of disease and ailments in the living populations as per our survey samples in Delhi and Jammu. Kashmir has been left out of this section, as enough data could not be generated on this aspect due to special difficulties of fieldwork there.

(a) DELHI (Tables V a & b, VII and VIII a &b)

In a population of 1277, 105 (8.2%) reported suffering from various ailments. Of these (46.7%) were males and 56 (53.3%) were females. Among the 105 sick the major problems were diabetes (26.7%), hypertension (19.0%), cardiac problems (9.5%), depression (15.2%), thyroid problem (5.7%), bronchitis, arthritis and gastric disorders (4.8% each) and ten individuals suffered from miscellaneous (Table IV b) ailments (9.5%).

The graph rises as we go up the age table 0-14 age group does not show any problem, in the 15-29 age group there are mere 3 (2.8%) cases and in 30-44 age grade there are just 9 (8.6%) suffering from different ailments. But there is a sharp rise in the incidence of persons with health problems with 39 (37.1%) cases in the 45-59 age group which goes up further at the 60 plus level with 54 (51.1%) cases.

More men suffer from diabetes and cardiac problems but more women are prone to depression and hypertension. Children apparently are receiving good attention regarding their healthcare as no cases of illness have been reported in the 0-14 age group.

(b) JAMMU (Tables VI a & b, VII and VIII a & b)

Our Jammu survey sample constitutes a population of 1706 of whom 894 are males and 812 are females. Of the 75 people reported suffering from various diseases 32 (3.6% of the male population) are males and 43 (5.3% of the female population) are females. Among the notable diseases are depression (13.3% cases), cardiac problems (22.7% cases) followed by diabetes (12.0% cases) miscellaneous diseases (12.0% cases), gastric problems (8.0% cases) bronchitis (6.7% cases) and arthritis (5.3% cases). Among the sick 42.7% are males and 57.3% females. Heart disease is a major worry for women while depression is nearly evenly distributed between the two sexes. Also women outnumber men as victims of all other diseases. Naturally, the burden of ill health is heavier on women as compared to men under the difficult circumstances of life in exile even more than a decade after the event. However, all round indications — as per available data presented in this chapter — are that children's health and nutrition is being taken proper care of in all the three regions of Delhi, Jammu and Kashmir.

There does seem to be a degree of under-reporting of the presence of various health problems especially those ailments which are not life threatening but only contribute to making day to day living a little more troublesome and vexatious. When we qualified our questions regarding 'health problems' with the word 'serious' it seems our informants tended to exclude problems such as impaired hearing, impaired vision, high and low blood pressure, body aches of various kinds, etc. Also, we noticed a certain reluctance to talk too much about women's health matters.

Besides, under the difficult conditions of 'camp life' after everything has turned topsy turvy, the attitude is to ignore any minor signs of ill-health so long one is able to move around and attend to one's work without too much discomfort. Tliis attitude and perception are a product of the after effects of the collective trauma caused by the uprooting of the community from its moorings during 1989-90.

It was not merely a question of losing one's property and the means of livelihood but also disruption of the rhythm of social-cultural life. When an entire community gets scattered and then transplanted - under forced circumstances - its world view and outlook and understanding of their day to day existence undergoes changes and modifications — some subtle, some not so subtle - in the process of adjustment to the changed circumstances.

Table I
Deaths After Migration: Delhi (1990*2002)

Cause of death	*Depression*		*Cardiac problems*		*Brain haemm.*		*Cancer*		*Diabetes*		*Natural deaths*		*Old age paralysis*		*Sunstroke*		*Misc.*		*Total*		***Grand Total***
Sex	*male*	*female*	*male*	*female*	*male*	*female*	*male*	*female*	*male*	*female*	*male*	*female*	*male*	*female*	*male*	*female*	*male*	*female*	*male*	*female*	
Age cohorts																					
0-14	0	0	0	0	0	0	0	0	0	0	0	0	0	0	0	0	0	0	0	0	0
15-29	1	0	0	1	0	0	0	0	0	0	0	0	0	0	0	0	0	1	1	2	3
30-44	2	0	0	0	0	0	1	0	0	0	0	0	0	0	0	0	2	0	5	0	5
45-59	4	5	1	2	2	0	1	0	0	0	1	2	0	0	1	0	0	0	10	9	19
60 and above	13	13	13	9	2	0	6	2	5	2	3	1	.6	2	2	3	3	0	53	32	85
Subtotal	20	18	14	12	4	0	8	2	5	2	4	3	6	2	3	3	5	1	69	43	112
TOTAL	38		26		4			10	7		7		8		6		6		112		112

* Misc. includes causes like accident (1), bronchitis (2), snake bite (1) and kidney problems (2)

Table II
Deaths After Migration: Jammu (1990-2002)

Cause of death	*Cancer*		*Depression*		*Diabetes*		*Cardiac*		*Natural*		*Kidney*		*Sunstroke*		*Bronchitis*		*Accident*		*Misc.*		*Total*		*Grand Total*
Sex	*male*	*fe-male*	*male*	*fe-mak*	*male*	*fe-male*	*male*	*fe-male*	*male*	*fe-male*	*male*	*fe-male*	*male*	*female*	*male*	*fe-male*	*male*	*fe-male*	*male*	*fe-male*	*male*	*fe-male*	
Age cohorts																							
0-14	0	0	0	0	0	0	0	0	0	1	0	0	0	0	0	0	0	3	0	0	0	4	4
15-29	0	0	1	0	0	0	0	0	0	0	1	0	0	0	0	0	0	1	0	0	2	1	3
30-44	2	0	1	0	0	1	1	0	1	0	2	0	1	0	0	0	2	0	0	6	10	7	17
45-59	1	2	3	0	2	1	1	4	3	2	1	0	0	1	0	1	1	0	0	2	12	13	25
60 and above	4	2	1	5	3	9	5	6	14	10	2	0	5	3	5	1	0	0	7	5	46	41	87
Subtotal	7	4	6	5	5	11	7	10	18	13	6	0	6	4	5	2	3	4	7	13	70	66	136
Total	11		11		16		17		31		6		10		7		7		20		136		136

Table III
Deaths: Kashmir Valley (1990-2002)

Cause of death	*Bronchitis*		*Cardiac problems*		*Intestinal problem*		*Cancer*		*Natural deaths*		*Accident*		*•Misc.*		*Total*		*Grand Total*
Sex	*male*	*female*	*male*	*fenale*	*male*	*female*	*male*	*female*	*male*	*female*	*male*	*female*	*male*	*female*	*male*	*female*	
Age cohorts																	
0-14	0	0	0	0	0	0	0	0	0	0	0	0	0	0	0	0	0
15-29	1	0	0	0	0	1	1	0	0	0	0	1	1	1	3	3	6
30-44	0	0	0	0	0	0	1	2	0	0	1	0	0	0	2	2	4
45-59	1	1	0	0	0	0	2	0	4	1	0	0	1	1	8	3	11
60 and above	3	3	5	1	2	4	7	2	11	8	2	1	4	2	34	21	55
Subtotal	5	4	5	1	2	5	11	4	15	9	3	2	6	4	47	29	
Total	9		6		7		15		24		5		10		7		76

*Misc. includes causes like accident (1), bronchitis(2),snake bite and kidney problems(2)

Table V [a]
Health Problems: Delhi

Disease	*Diabetes*		*Hypertension*		*Arthritis*		*Bronchitis*		*Depression*		*Cardiac*		*Thyroid*		*Gastric*		**Misc.*		*Total*		*Grand Total*
Sex	*male*	*female*	*male*	*female*	*male*	*female*	*male*	*female*	*male*	*female*	*male*	*female*	*male*	*female*	*male*	*female*	*male*	*female*	*male*	*female*	
Age cohorts																					
0-14	.0	0	0	0	0	0	0	0	0	0	0	0	0	0	0	0	0	0	0	0	0
15-29	0	1	0	0	0	0	0	0	0	0	0	0	0	0	0	0	1	1	1	2	3
30-44	3	0	0	1	0	1	1	0	0	0	1	0	1	0	0	0	1	0	7	2	9
45-59 .	6	6	2	4	0	2	0	0	2	7	2	0	2	3	0	0	1	2	15	24	39
60 and above	7	5	5	8	0	2	2	2	3	4	5	2	0	0	2	3	2	2	26	28	54
Subtotal	16	12	7	13	0	5	3	2	5	11	8	2	3	3	2	3	5	5	49	56	105
Total	28		20		5		5			16	10		6		5		10		105		105

Table VI |a]
Health Problems: Jammu

Disease	*Depression*		*Cardiac*		*Diabetes*		*Bronchitis*		*Arthritis*		*Gastric*		*Misc.*		*TOTAL*		***Grand Total***
Sex	*male*	*female*	*male*	*female*	*male*	*female*	*male*	*female*	*male*	*female*	*male*	*female*	*male*	*female*	*male*	*female*	
Age cohorts																	
0-14	0	0	**0**	**0**	**0**	**0**	0	0	0	0	0	0	0	0	0	0	0
15-29	0	0	**0**	**1**	**1**	**0**	**0**	**0**	0	1	0	0	2	0	3	2	5
30-44	2	12	**0**	**2**	**1**	**1**	**0**	**0**	**0**	**0**	0	0	2	0	5	15	20
45-59	0	**1**	**2**	**3**	**1**	**1**	**0**	**1**	**1**	**1**	**1**	**3**	0	1	5	11	16
60 and above	10	0	**4**	**5**	**1**	**3**	**2**	**2**	**0**	**1**	**1**	**1**	**1**	**3**	19	15	34
Subtotal	12	13	6	11	4	5	2	3	1	3	2	4	5	4	32	43	75
TOTAL	25		17		9		5		4		6		9		75		75

Table V[b]
Health Problems: Delhi

Miscellaneous Health Problems		
Diseases	*Sex*	*Age (in years)*
Meningitis	M	17
Mentally retarded	M	30
Cirrhosis	M	55
Spinal problem	M	65
Kidney problem	M	70
Paralysis	F	20
Low fever	F	54
Skin disease	F	59
Cataract	F	62
Gynae problems	F	65

Table VI [b]
Health Problems: Jammu

Miscellaneous Health Problems		
Diseases	*Sex*	*Age (in years)*
Polio	M	19
Mentally retarded	M	27
Kidney problems	M	40
Hearing problem	M	42
Sciatica	M	60
Sciatica	F	60
Gynecological	F	50
Paralysis	F	62
Skin	F	65
Cataract	F	66

Table VII
Overall Health Status

Disease	*Delhi*			*Jammu*			*Total*		
	Male	*Female*	*Total*	*Male*	*Female*	*Total*	*Male*	*Female*	*Total*
Diabetes	16	12	28	4	5	9	20	17	37
Depression	5	11	16	2	3	5	7	14	21
Cardiac problem	8	20	28	6	11	17	14	31	45
Bronchitis	3	2	5	2	3	5	5	5	10
Thyroid	3	3	6	0	0	0	3	3	6
Intestinal problem	2	3	5	2	4	6	4	7	11
BP	7	13	20	0	0	0	7	13	20
Arthritis	0	5	5	1	3	4	1	8	9
Total	44	69	113	17	29	46	61	98	159

Table VIII (a)
Health Problems: Delhi & Jammu

Region	*Delhi*			*Jammu*			*Total*		
Population	*1277*			*1760*			*2983*		
Disease	*M*	*F*	*M+F*	*M*	*F*	*M+F*	*M*	*F*	*M+F*
Diabetes	16	12	28	4	5	9	20	17	37
Depression	5	11	16	12	13	25	17	24	41
Cardiac	8	2	10	6	11	17	14	13	27
Bronchitis	3	2	5	2	3	5	5	5	10
Gastric	2	3	5	2	4	6	4	7	11
Thyroid	3	3	6	0	0	0	3	3	6
Hypertension	7	13	20	0	0	0	7	13	20
Arthritis	0	5	5	1	3	4	1	8	9
Miscella-neous	5	5	10	5	4	9	10	9	19
Total	49	56	105	32	43	75	81	99	180

Table VIII(b)

Region	*Delhi*			*Jammu*			*Total*		
	M	*F*	*M+F*	*M*	*F*	*M+F*	*M*	*F*	*M+F*
No. with ailments	49	56	105	32	43	75	81	99	180
Population	647	630	1277	894	812	1706	1541	1442	2983
Percentage of sick	7.6	8.9	8.2	3.6	5.3	4.4	5.2	6.8	6.0

CHAPTER – 6

PATH OF RECONSTRUCTION

Like everywhere else in the world when people feel forced to abandon their homes, Kashmiri Pandits as a community suffered deep anguish and trauma on having to leave Kashmir Valley - their home for millennia - under most unfortunate and unforseen circumstances. Their suffering has been physical, mental, and economic. These are well known facts of recent Kashmir history but what we are attempting in this report is to substantiate the story in its various aspects in a graphic and cogent manner on the basis of the data and views gathered from the people themselves.

Our main concern in this chapter is to see that after twelve years of the traumatic experience, what has the uprooted Kashmiri Pandit community done to rehabilitate itself readjust and reconstruct its life on the path towards the present well-being and future progress.

In this context we tried to look for some indicators, some material evidence in support of their resilient endeavours to move on in life. Through interviews and through our schedule (questionnaire) we tried to know from each household about the kind of property artefacts they had acquired post migration (see Table I). The answers we got were collectively reassuring. That is, in spite of the disastrous economic losses and loss or diminution of their jobs and the heavy burden of starting from scratch in unfamiliar and unhelpful circumstances, these people have caught on the reality head on and struggled to regain the normal rhvthm of life for themselves, men and women, old and young, and their growing children.

Table I (A & B) shows that 215 (36.4%) households had acquired their own houses/flats and 70 (12%) households had bought house plots. We are talking only about the migrants settled in Delhi and Jammu. Kashmiri Pandits still in Kashmir Valley are not migrants as they are mostly living in their own houses and holding on to whatever jobs have been theirs. But the information relating to them in Table I is there only for comparison.

As we go further down the list under Delhi and Jammu columns in the Table, we observe that 88% households have television/cassette player-cum radio etc. as an easily accessible home entertainment facility for the benefit of all family members. A refrigerator for food storage and cold water in hot weather conditions are top priority items for purchase for 75% households. In comparison only 6.5% households in our Kashmir Valley sample have refrigerators because of the cool/cold climatic conditions there. But 69% homes have television and music players, as these facilities are necessary (and also affordable) for news and entertainment

However, when we compare Delhi group and Jammu group with each other, we find that the former is much more prosperous as indicated by the quantity and distribution of the property items acquired post-migration. In Delhi, 72% households have acquired houses/flats and about 16% house plots. In Jammu only 10% and 9% households have got houses and house plots, respectively. Besides, 71% families have telephones, 83% have refrigerators and nearly half of them (48%) also have washing machines in Delhi. More than one third families in Delhi also have a car or a motorbike/scooter, while only 12% have this facility in our Jammu sample and 10% families in Kashmir. Eighteen families in Delhi also have pet dogs, one in Jammu, and nine in Kashmir (may be for security reasons). As we have seen in the chapter on employment Delhi offers much better chances and opportunities for employment (especially in the private sector), which have been availed of by the migrants. By all indications and facts gathered in this study they are better employed and relatively more prosperous generally. Hence, their capacity for acquiring more things among more households.

On our inquiry about the source of their financial investment on the acquired items especially houses/flats and house plots etc. we are informed about the various sources of money invested i.e.,

(a) Some families had been able to sell their houses/ house plots/agricultural/ horticultural lands etc. in Kashmir. The prices they had received were mostly well below the market value prevailing in Kashmir Valley but they had no choice.

(b) Some had gone for loans from private agencies, banks or employers and purchases were made on instalment basis.

(c) Some had used their savings in cash and securities in banks etc. to acquire items considered essential for return to attainable normalcy and for future progress and well-being.

Whatever planning they have obviously done in fixing their priorities in terms of overall assessment of the situation and for making their lives a little more pleasant does make a lot of sense.

Table I
Property Acquired
Post Migration (Household -Wise)

	Delhi 'A'		*Jammu 'B'*		*A+B*	*Kashmir 'C**		*Total*	
Total No. of House-holds	*250*		*340*			*153*		*743*	
House/Flat	181	72.40%	34	10.00%	36%	108	70.59%	323	43.47%
House plot	39	15.60%	31	9.12%	12%	66	43.14%	136	18.30%
Telephone	177	70.80%	82	24.12%	44%	17	11.11%	276	37.15%
Refrigerator	208	83.20%	235	69.12%	75%	.10	6,54%	453	60.97%
T. V., Music	231	92.40%	289	85.00%	88%	105	68.63%	625	84.12%
Washing Machine	121	48.40%	27	7.94%	25%	6	3.92%	154	20.73%
Car/Scooter	90	36.00%	41	12.06%	22%	15	9.80%	146	19.65%
Pet dog	18	7.20%	1	0.29%	3%	9	5.88%	28	3.77%
Gold ornament	158	63.20%	165	48.53%	55%	0	0.00%	323	43.47%
Any other	1	0.40%	72	21.18%	12%	1	0.65%	74	9.96%

CHAPTER – 7

PROPERTY LOSSES

Before Jammu and Kashmir, the state of Punjab had been the scene of militancy and terrorism on a large scale. There was considerable loss of life when the extremists killed Hindus in towns and villages. In many places the insecure atmosphere caused the Hindus and some Sikhs also to leave Punjab and move to Delhi and other places (they later returned to their homes after normalcy was restored in Punjab). In many places there was destruction and loss of property of the Hindus, but while the loss of life among the Kashmiri Pandits in Kashmir was much less in absolute terms, than what the Punjabi Hindus suffered at the hands of the extremists in Punjab the destruction and loss of property of the Kashmiri Pandits on the whole and as the average per household has been far too heavier and extensive. For the vast majority of the Kashmiri Pandit migrants the losses have been total and very marginally retrievable if at all, by way of distress sales of the property (at prices far below the market prices). Most of these sales were negotiated and settled after migration from Kashmir when the owners had no effective control over the property and/or were partially or fully destroyed e.g., houses, with household goods and shops with stocks for sale, trees, cattle (in villages), residential plots, agricultural lands, plantations etc. along with their produce. However, in the vast majority of cases the houses, house plots and lands remain unsold.

In our sample of 743 households surveyed in Jammu (340), Delhi (250) and Kashmir (153), the heaviest losses have been reported by the migrants staying in the camps in the Jammu region. The average loss per household here is 22.7 lakhs (see Table I). Three hundred and twenty six (326) families have lost their houses worth 2,347 lakhs, 92 families have left behind house plots (land) worth 349 lakhs and shops (with merchandise) worth about 636 lakhs have been lost by 105 households. Household goods worth nearly 809 lakhs were left behind by 308 families, and of these no trace could be found later. Two hundred and eighty eight families owned productive agricultural/horticultural land worth about 2672 lakhs almost all of it in the countryside, but has been lying waste for the owners since their exodus. And maybe in some places the lands might have been encroached upon or utilised by other people for their own benefit. But, of course, that would not affect the legal ownership of the property. However, the usefulness of the landed property as very valuable sources of food grains, vegetables, trees and fodder for cattle etc. has not been available and accessible to the owners since the days of their migration. The trees have been mostly cut away and the abandoned cattle taken over by other people.

Average per household loss reported by our sample of250 households in Delhi is 10.37 lakhs. The major properties lost are houses shops, and house plots worth about 1200 lakhs. Also household goods and agricultural land worth 217 lakhs have been left behind. Besides, miscellaneous items worth 1065 lakhs have also been lost by them.

Even in Kashmir Valley where the Kashmiri Pandit families, who have stayed on have lost properties worth 269 lakhs. That is so because the militants and their friends have selectively burnt houses and shops, looted abandoned houses and business establishments, destroyed temples and grain stores, taken away cattle and trees at their will. So some Hindus still staying on in Kashmir have had to move away from one place to another for better relative security or for job requirements etc. However, such faith in relative security has sometimes proved illusory and disastrous Disasters like (a) Sangrampura, (Budgam: March 1997) when seven Pandits were killed, (b) at Wandahama, (Srinagar: January (1998) when 23 Pandits were shot dead by the terrorists and (c) at Nadimarg (Pulwama: March 2003) when 24 Pandits were massacred by the terrorists, and a series of minor incidents besides have been evidence to the contrary.

COMPENSATION

In the face of such heavy losses, we tried to find out if they had received any compensation from the state government or insurance companies (wherever the properties were insured against damage or loss). The Jammu families reported that 51 families had received an amount of about 256 lakhs for loss of their houses and a house plot; another family had received a lakh as insurance money for the loss of its car. The above money had come from both the government sources (at the flat rate of 1 lakh per house burnt and destroyed) and insurance companies. But many families in the countryside had not insured their properties at all. Only 12 households in our Delhi sample had received a compensation of 2.19 lakhs against loss of their houses. Some said their applications and claims were still pending with the state government and the insurance company offices at Jammu/Srinagar and they were finding it difficult to pursue the cases for lack of time, and the bribes demanded at both places by the junior officials. The Kashmiri Pandit families still living in Kashmir did not report having received any compensation for any damage to their property.

Post 1990, after the exodus from Kashmir a small number of households, out of a feeling of despair in a situation that inspired little hope of returning, tried to dispose of their properties still lying intact in their old locations in Kashmir. There was also the great and urgent need for finances for meeting the demands of the new situation and resettlement needs. Most of these sales had to be distress sales at much below market prices but money was badly needed.

Even in Kashmir Valley 6 families had sold their houses for 35 lakhs in all in Delhi only 3 households reported the sale of their houses (or house plots) at a total cost of 15 lakhs. But most probably here people were not eager to talk about this very freely or frankly. Some were still in the process of taking a final decision in the matter and most of them wanted to wait for some more time and watch the developments. Selling one's home and hearth and ancestral property and in the process snapping one's ties with one's village/town/homeland and one's roots is never an easy decision to make. It is absolutely heart-breaking!

The Jammu families reported a little action in this context About 12 households had sold their houses/house plots and shops for about 73 lakhs, and another 25 families had sold their agricultural land/cattle/trees for about 39 lakhs.

The overall impression we gathered during our enquiries and conversation with the migrant Kashmiri Pandits was that a vast majority of families have yet retained the legal ownership of their entire or at least part of their landed property, and homes and shops and homestead plots, wherever intact, because of (a) their deep sentimental feelings (b) no serious proposal for sale had been explored (c) in the hope that they may be able to return home under peaceful conditions in the foreseeable future. A political settlement with Pakistan could make that possible.

However, the members of the younger generation who have grown up and studied outside Kashmir Valley, and are working or hope to explore the wider and the more diversified job market all over India think of Kashmir as a home for holidays, and for work related involvements that would help develop Kashmir in future as an economically flourishing place with its beauty intact.

Table I
Estimated Value of Property Lost

Description of Property	*Estimated value*					
	Jammu (3400 Households)		*Delhi (250 Households)*		*Kashmir (153 Households)*	
	Rs. In lakhs	*No. of households*	*Rs. In lakhs*	*No. of households*	*Rs. In lakhs*	*No. of households*
House/Flat	2346.98	326	1156.00	99	148.65	41
House/Plot	349.06		28.00	5	1.00	1
Shop/Factory	635.83	105	15.00	5	6.00	2
Household goods	808.70	308	26.00	2	47.00	19
Agriculture/Horticultural land	2672.50	288	291.35	17	0.00	0
Cattle/Trees	675.71	248	0.50	1	10.00	7
Cash/Valuables in a Bank/ Locker or in private custody	36.64	13	4.80	4	0.00	0
Any vehicle	37.68	22	36.00	3	9.00	3
Any other item	102.25	141	1029.00	68	46.40	20
2nd other item	52.20	74	6.00	1	0.92	2
Total	7717.53	–	2592.65	–	268.97	–
Average Loss Per Household	Rs. 22.7		Rs. 10.37		Rs. 1.58	

* Value in lakhs

Table II
Relief Received from Govt. Insurance Company Etc.

Description of Property	*Relief Received from Govt Including Govt Compensation and Insurance Money for House etc.*					
	Jammu		*Delhi*		*Kashmir*	
	Rs. in lakhs	*No. of house-holds*	*Rs. in lakhs*	*No. of house-holds*	*Rs. in lakhs*	*No. of house-holds*
House/Flat	254.74	50	2.19	12	0.00	0
House/Plot	1.00	1	0.00	0	0.00	0
Shop/Factory	0.00	0	0.00	0	0.00	0
Household goods	0.00	0	0.00	0	0.00	0
Agriculture / Horticultural land	0.00	0	0.00	0	0.00	0
Cattle/Trees	0.00	0	0.00	0	0.00	0
Cash/Valuables in a Bank/ Locker or in private custody	0.00	0	0.00	0	0.00	0
Any vehicle	1.00	1	0.00	0	0.00	0
Any other item	0.00	0	0.00	0	0.00	0
2nd other item	0.35	9	0.00	0	0.00	0

* Value in lakhs

Table III
Value of Property Sold

Description of Property	*Sold before or after migration*					
	Jammu		*Delhi*		*Kashmir*	
	Rs. in lakhs	*No. of households*	*Rs. in lakhs*	*No. of house-holds*	*Rs. in lakhs*	*No. of households*
House/Flat	71.30	9	15.00	3	35.00	6
House/Plot	0.20	1	0.00	0	0.00	0
Shop/Factory	1.29	2	0.00	0	0.00	0
Household goods	0.35	1	0.00	0	0.00	0
Agriculture/Horticultural land	34.40	16	0.00	0	0.00	0
Cattle/Trees	4.42	9	0.00	0	0.00	0
Cash/Valuables in a Bank Locker or in private custody	0.00	0	0.00	0	0.00	0
Any vehicle	0.15	1	0.00	0	0.00	0
Any other item	0.00	0	0.00	0	35.00	5
2°° other item	5.21	6	0.02 -	1	0.00	0

* Value in lakhs

Chapter – 8

AGONY OF WOMEN AND CHILDREN: THE VULNERABLE AND THE INNOCENT

From time immemorial, when an invading and conquering army enters a new territory the women of the subjugated people become the special targets of exploitation and abuse at its hands. Women in a very special way personify the sentiments of honour and self-respect in the collective consciousness of a community, a country, and a nation. So any acts of disrespect and dishonour directed towards them constitute a very effective way of humiliating the targeted people. Also, these give a sense of power to the perpetrators of such cruel and crude behaviour, their minds already coarsened by mindless violent acts of war or terrorism. The children too, being a very vulnerable and innocent section of society, become easy targets of cruelty and exploitation in such situations.

In the late eighties, conditions in the Valley were slowly ripening towards a situation of conflict and violence leading to a proxy war unleashed by the militants, mutating as terrorists, against the State and against all agencies and groups perceived to be pro-India and supportive of the official establishment and policies. The Kashmiri Pandits were one such group. Their population was small (barely 5%) but significant in terms of their being native Kashmiris and a well educated and moderately well off group, totally committed to the Indian position and the rule of law in Kashmir. Also they were spread across the Valley in the remote villages, towns, and the city of Srinagar (a large section was concentrated here). Many of them were holding government posts (at junior and senior levels) in the state and central government offices. They, therefore, became an easy and natural target.

The hostile elements in Kashmir are the Islamic Jehadi groups (known by various names) guided, supported, trained, and equipped by Pakistan to help it create conditions for annexation of Kashmir. There are some other groups who claim to be fighting for an independent Kashmir but they also have been receiving help and material assistance from Pakistan. For all these groups, the pro-India Kashmiri Pandits have been targets for hostility and violence and for vicious propaganda. The state of terror created against them finally led to their mass exodus from the Valley in 1989-1990.

In the late eighties, as the political and social atmosphere in the Valley started hotting up through agitations, processions, *bandhs,* and anti-government and anti India slogans, it became clear that the political leadership in the state, civil authorities and the police force had taken a back seat, while the militants, openly expressing pro-Azadi and pro-Pakistan sentiments had gained the upper hand. In this charged atmosphere, it was not surprising that Kashmiri Pandits were cautioned and warned and felt threatened. One slogan that received some currency those days was, *Asi kya gachi - Pakistan; Batao ros ta Batnyao saan* (we want Pakistan with Pandit women, but without Pandit men). Small groups of hot-headed young men equipped with AK-47 rifles, hand grenades, land mines and deadly explosives, quite often led and guided by Pakistani Jehadis, spread across the Valley executing their secret mission of selective destruction of public property, security apparatus and the temples and houses of Hindus. They started selectively killing Kashmiri Pandit men, women and children. The odd killings started way back in 1987, 1988 and 1989, but the execution of the innocent reached a climax in the year 1990. As per the information painstakingly gathered by the Panun Kashmir Movement (Raina, 2004: 77-94, 313-315), between February and September 1990, three hundred and eleven (311) Kashmiri Pandits were killed in the Valley by terrorists belonging to different outfits. Out of these, 18 were women (see Table I), including 3 very young unmarried girls (sl. nos. 5, 10, & 13). Babli (sl. no. 11) was killed along with her mother and Girija (sl. no. 12) along with both her parents. Subsequently, more men and some children were killed in Doda, Udhampur, and Anantnag districts during 1993, 1995, 1997, and 2000. Besides, there were major massacres at (a) village Sangrampura, Budgam district on March 21, 1997 with 7 men killed, (b) Wandhama, Srinagar district on 26th of January, 1998 with 23 persons killed that included 10 women (6 girls and 4 married women), (c) Nadimarg, Anantnag - Pulwama district on March 23, 2003 with 24 persons killed that included 11 women (5 girls 6 married women) and two little male babies (less than 2 years of age) in their mothers' laps (see Table II); (the detailed particulars given here are drawn from the project data).

As listed in the above-referred book, between April 3,1987 and March 23, 2003, 383 Kashmiri Hindus were killed in all, most of them in the Valley and a few in Jammu. This included men, women, and children. In all 40 women (see Tables I & II), including 14 unmarried girls, were killed. Quite a few among the dead are believed to be children (both male and female). The details are, however, lacking. But regarding the Nadimarg massacre the details provided are based on the project data.

All the affected families had been surveyed by us in December 2002 about four months before the terrorists struck in March 2003. These families had braved it out there for 13 years after the Exodus. Then their faith and trust in human goodness was betrayed! Among the dead were two little male babies in their young mothers' laps. All of them, including the little babies, were shot dead on that fateful dark night. Three other confirmed cases of children's death are mentioned in the book (ibid). One is that of a boy's dead body found floating in the Jhelum on May 10, 1990 (S. No. 89, p. 81). The other is that of the minor son of one Jia Lal Kaw; both father and son were kidnapped and killed at Handwara on May 18, 1990 (S. Nos. 200 & 201, p. 86). Then there is the case of a young girl Babli, a student who was killed together with her mother, Rupawati, a housewife, on July 1, 1990 at Handwara (see Table I, sl. nos. 10 & 11). Surely there must be other cases of children having been killed but in the absence of detailed information we are unable to identify them.

There was no single method of killing the potential victims — men and women. Some were simply shot down. This proved to be the most merciful mode of killing adopted. One of the earliest victims was a Hindu nurse at Sher- E-Kashmir Institute of Medical Sciences, Srinagar. She had been a witness to some wounded terrorists getting unauthorised treatment in the hospital. She was kidnapped, tied to a tree and killed in a very cruel manner. Girija, a lady teacher, was kidnapped, raped and sawn into pieces on a mechanical saw at Bandipora while still alive. Prana Ganjoo, a college teacher was kidnapped, raped, and killed along with her husband, also a college teacher at Sopore on May 7,1990. Girija Dhar, a young girl, was killed along with her parents in Srinagar on July 1, 1990.

A young man, Brij Nath Kaul, a government employee, was picked up from his residence in Anantnag district by the terrorists on June 26, 1990 and taken away. His wife ran after them, begging for her husband's release but to no avail. Both of them were tied to the rear of a vehicle and dragged along till they died. Their battered bodies were found lying 10 kms away on the road. Some people were killed and bodies thrown into the nearest river. There are also reported cases of men and children being thrown alive into rivers and drowned. In some instances, drowning persons were pushed back to midstream when they tried to come ashore, till they were drowned (Anantnag district). In most cases victims were tortured in various ways before being killed. Some were beheaded, some strangulated and in one case hands and feet were chopped off. In another case Brij Nath Shah of Kupwara was killed and his body hung on a tree with his lips stitched (April 27, 1990). Three LIC officials were sought to be burnt alive in a locked house (left behind by a migrated family). Two died and one escaped with 50% burns (ibid: 160-163).

As per the above-referred information, 54% of the persons killed were in Srinagar district, 16% in Anantnag district and the remaining 30% were in the districts of Budgam, Baramula, Pulwama and Kupwara. There is a good reason for the fact that more than half the people killed belonged to Srinagar district. About half the total population of Kashmiri Pandits was concentrated in Srinagar city and its immediate environs and suburbs. Besides, Srinagar city is the nerve centre of the militant and terrorist activities and of separatist politics.

At this point a note of caution is called for. Not for a moment are we suggesting that the vast majority of the Kashmiri Muslims approved of or was directly involved in the unprovoked violent outrages against the hapless unarmed Hindu minority. But the silent majority preferred to remain silent and saw the happenings with an unseeing eye! At the same time we should remember that the fear of the gun in the hands of reckless and strongly motivated individuals can be a truly benumbing and scary experience for ordinary peace loving citizens. Besides, there were no rewards except at the purely human and moral planes for going out of the way to court danger to protect the Hindus.

In course of our investigation, quite a number of our informants told us that there were occasions when a Muslim neighbour, friend, colleague or an acquaintance took care to caution, advise and help them in dealing with potential danger and threat and even in the arrangements for escaping to safety. For example:

1. **Schedule No. 236:** (Pulwama) Her cousin was abducted and beaten badly. She too was threatened. Brother had a good job, he stayed back; terrorists came to kill him but the Muslim neighbour came to his rescue and saved him.
2. **Schedule No. 46:** (Kupwara) His son (a teacher) was saved from being kidnapped by terrorists by a Muslim friend, while returning home from school.
3. **Schedule No. 107:** (Kupwara) His old father and seven uncles were lined up and shot dead on the same day. Migrated to Jammu but returned after some time; found the atmosphere changed for the worse, almost hostile. So went back to Jammu but during their brief stay in their own house in Kashmir a Muslim friend (a teacher) also slept in the same house to safeguard their lives and to guarantee their safety till they returned to Jammu.
4. **Schedule No. 342:** (Budgam) Threatening letters received. Muslim neighbours advised them to leave, even helped with the transport arrangements.

5. **Schedule No 55:** (Kupwara) Her elder son (25 years) was suspected to be an informer (of government agencies) by the militants. As such he was reported to be on their hit list. Their Muslim friends cautioned them about the danger and so they migrated to Jammu.

But here are some variations on this theme

6. **Schedule No. 587:** (Srinagar) Their home in Srinagar district was near an army petrol depot and thus they had some degree of security. Besides, their Muslim neighbours had assured them of support for their safety. But after six months, a Hindu neighbour was killed by the terrorists. At that point, the Muslim neighbours conveyed their inability to stand by their assurances. So they decided to leave in October 1990.
7. **Schedule No. 249:** A Hindu employee of the veterinary department came to their village to meet a Muslim colleague (cashier). Together they went to another village where their office was located, so that the former could collect his salary. The Muslim colleague persuaded him to stay there overnight as it was getting late. Next morning, the terrorists came and took him to the premises of a local mosque. They ordered him to make a rope out of some grass lying around. Then he was asked to tie the rope to the branch of a walnut tree and hang himself with it. At this point, he begged for mercy, offered to give all his property to them if his life was spared. He had a wife and three daughters to take care of. But to no avail. He was hanged to death, while a whole crowd of local inhabitants laughed and jeered at this macabre scene.

Throughout the world, across the ages, human beings and human societies and cultures have vainly struggled against the sharp duality of human nature: to seek the path of peace and compassion in human affairs, and at the same time to indulge in actions of violence and cruelty towards fellow human beings for causes and concerns invented and nurtured by themselves and to draw satisfaction and pleasure out of such violence. No animal species has shown such enormous propensity for self-destruction.

The violence in Kashmir, whether unleashed by religious zealots mostly to serve their narrow religious purposes and/or the political objectives of another country or pursued by the security forces in retaliatory action in defence of the state, falls in the classical pattern described above. The outcome has been the same: all-round destruction, including the death of the innocent and violation of human rights and values. The resulting distortions in normal human relationships and behaviour patterns have led to developments of an abnormal kind e.g. the sudden exodus of a segment of the population, sharp rise in the incidence of mental disease in the population, creation of a large population of widows and orphans and parents minus their young sons, most of the youth were involved in scrounging for elusive assurances of security or labouring for the evening meal. And there was the onerous task of protecting their womenfolk and children from all possible dangers.

In the course of our investigations and interviews, Kashmiri Pandit migrants invariably stated that one of the most important reasons for them to leave the Valley was to "protect the honour of our womenfolk and the security and safety of our children and elders." This statement is recorded in many schedules in Delhi and Jammu. To quote a few:

1. **Schedule No. 439:** (district Srinagar) "There were reports of kidnapping of KP girls and even their being killed or lost to their families. The kidnapped girls never returned home."

2. **Schedule No. 417:** (district Srinagar) "Concern for honour and security was the main reason for migration. We sent our daughters to Jammu earlier as there were many reports of girls being kidnapped. The militants were even asking for KP boys to join and train with them for terrorist activities."
3. **Schedule No. 423:** (district Anantnag) "In the atmosphere of all round insecurity women's dignity was in danger. Relatives had been killed and their slogan - We want Pakistan here minus KP men but with KP women - was ominous."
4. **Schedule No. 577:** (district Srinagar) "Due to reports of some young women (KP) having been kidnapped in their area and fear psychology created by the terrorists proclaiming their desire to establish Nizam - e - Mustafa in Kashmir, they left the Valley."
5. **Schedule No. 536:** (Kupwara)"My cousin was kidnapped and killed, neighbour shot dead and uncle was poisoned. Also, neighbourhood girls were humiliated and insulted by the militants. So we migrated."
6. **Schedule No. 525:** (Srinagar city) "A KP girl in our neighbourhood was raped by the militants in front of her family."

Amidst the general mayhem and lawlessness, an atmosphere of violence against the Hindus was being generated and nursed with abandon. There was no serious opposition from the weak and demoralised administrative machinery, which lacked direction and the will to meet the challenge that the situation posed. The atmosphere was getting hotter and hotter in 1989 and the lid was off after the release of jailed JKLF militants following the Rubaiya Sayeed episode on December 13, 1989. In the next few months a large number of Kashmiri Pandit men, women, and some young boys and girls were killed. But even before these killings occurred (May 1990 onwards) the main exodus had happened (March-April 1990) and continued through the year.

It has been alleged that the large-scale migration of Kashmiri Pandits in 1990 from the Valley to Jammu was because of the "informal advice" conveyed to that effect by Jagmohan, the then Governor of Jammu and Kashmir. The move was supposed to be temporary, as he was likely to take very stringent action against the militants and terrorist outfits and did not want the Kashmiri Pandits to suffer from possible reprisals from the latter and during operations to be launched against them by the security forces. The relief measures announced by him for the migrant families were described as an incentive, to encourage large- scale migration of the Hindu minority from the Valley. But, on the basis of our investigation and enquiry, we have come to the conclusion that there is no substance in this theory. Out of the hundreds of KP migrants that we interviewed not a single person made even a passing reference to this story. The developments in the Valley were warming up since the year 1986. They became hotter and hotter in 1988-89, and then boiled over in 1990. The actions of the terrorists and militants spawned extreme fear among the Hindus and their sense of absolute insecurity received confirmation from the ineffectiveness of the state administration in countering the excesses of the former. This syndrome was repeated in subsequent massacres of Kashmiri Pandits at Wandhama in January 1998 and Nadimarg in March 2003. Nobody would leave his/her home and hearth and one's native place (home since eternity) just to fulfil the requirements of a vague scheme, allegedly coming from the head of the State. One would do so only for extremely compelling and concrete reasons that would pose a direct threat to life and limb. And that is precisely what happened to the Kashmiri Pandits living in the Valley till 1989-1990 and even later.

Migration and After

Some families took the decision to leave the Valley after a bit of planning and were able to make reasonable arrangements to move out with some essential household goods - clothes, utensils and some important papers regarding their properties, bank accounts, educational certificates etc. But for the vast majority of families, moving out was like running away from a raging fire or desperately trying to keep their heads above the swirling waters of a cataclysmic flood. They had to leave in great haste to save their skins. In either situation, great secrecy had to be maintained to avoid the evil attention of the terrorists and their informers. Only highly trusted friends (both Hindus and Muslims) and close relatives were informed about their decision and help sought in making the basic arrangements like transport etc. Families did not always travel together to avoid suspicion. For greater safety, small groups of people travelled together but they would break up during the journey, if necessary.

Finding a shelter at Jammu was another ordeal. Some were lucky enough to get help from relatives and friends for temporary stay till any alternative accommodation could be arranged or provided by the government. Some people - men, women and children - had to spend days and nights under the trees in open spaces. Mothers had to be especially patient and use their ingenuity to cook meals to suit the needs and taste of their hungry children and the elders. In some instances, womenfolk had to travel alone, up and down, more than once, to bring back their little children left with relatives in Kashmir (at a supposedly safe place) and also to try to salvage some important item of their property left behind in a locked home under the general care of a Muslim neighbour or friend. Some of the men also made such attempts but quite often came back empty handed or did not come back at all. There is the case of a family, which left Srinagar for Delhi in September 1990, hoping to return soon when normalcy returned. They asked their next-door Muslim neighbour, who was generous with positive assurances, to keep an eye on their locked home. But, in November, he himself set the house on fire and informed the family about it on telephone, falsely blaming unknown terrorists/militants for the evil deed. In the subsequent weeks/months, there was confirmed evidence that he had removed to his own house all the household goods that included furniture and furnishings, clothes, utensils, books (a small library) etc. Not a scrap of paper could be retrieved after the loot. There have been many such cases in Srinagar and elsewhere in the Valley.

As the number of KP migrants kept swelling in the Jammu region several migrant camps were opened there and tents provided to the migrant families to stay in. In the scorching heat of a Jammu summer, the tents were like cauldrons of hell fire. There were no fans, no separate space for kitchens and no toilets or bathrooms. The women had to cook outside the tent and go out some distance to attend the call of nature. For taking a bath, they had to improvise but water remained a big problem even for drinking purposes. Inside the tent, a single room arrangement for the entire family, there was total lack of any privacy especially for young women, both married and unmarried, and for little girls and boys in their adolescent phase.

The older people were trying hard to keep their morale high in the face of extreme discomforts, but what hurt them most was having to make a daily display of the depredations of age on their withered and weathered bodies in front of the children and the younger family members and even neighbours. But these were abnormal times and they had to manage their lives somehow. Many of the older women could not speak Hindi or Dogri and faced a serious problem of communication with the local people and shopkeepers etc. but in due course this problem was overcome. For cooking and keeping warm during the wintry days sometimes women had to move around to collect dry grass and bits and pieces of wood to use as fuel. Some young men had to work as labourers *(mazdoors)* on a low daily wage to earn the evening's meal for the starving family.

Some unmarried girls had to enter into bogus marital arrangements with local young men to be able to get a ration card that would help them access relief measures provided by government agencies and NGOs. The conditions had indeed reached a point of desperation. These bogus 'husbands' later tried to exploit these young women, taking advantage of their helplessness. In some cases the arrangement reportedly ended up in real marriages but not happy ones most of the time.

The sudden influx of a large number of Kashmiri Hindus into Jammu city and other areas of the region caused a lot of anxiety and worry to the local people. The rumour was that the KP families were to get free plots of land for housing purposes and many of them would get government jobs as part of the relief arrangements. Also they thought that the Kashmiri Pandits, being a highly educated community, would give serious competition to local professionals like doctors, engineers, lawyers, and teachers etc. So there were protests and rumours at various levels and demands that the migrant professionals should not be allowed to practise at Jammu. Also there should not be any employment programmes for the KP young men and women in the State government departments and quasi-governmental organisations in the Jammu region and within the Jammu quota. If at all anyone had to seek employment he/she could do so only in the Kashmir quota. But even if selected (a doubtful proposition in most cases) there would be no question of any KP youth returning to Kashmir Valley under the prevailing circumstances. A KP family, now settled at Udhampur had approached J & K High Court on two occasions to question the legal validity of such restrictions (in terms of the Jammu and Kashmir and the Indian Constitutions) placed on the employment opportunities for the KP candidates while the community is facing such difficult times.

One thing is quite clear from our investigation. Beyond granting relief (in terms of the decisions taken by the government from time to time) there has been little effort to extend help in terms of a well thought out development plan to pull the community out of a grim situation of distress and penury in which history has placed it (for no fault of its own). Neither the state government nor the government of India has taken any initiative in this regard. For the first time in 2004 the Prime Minister of India Manmohan Singh visited the KP migrants at Jammu. He graciously announced that the one-room accommodation given to the migrants would be replaced by two room flats for each family. There was immediate reaction among some sections of the local population there. They wanted the government to distribute the migrant population living in the camps in Jammu region among various states of India. Apparently, having been pushed out of the Valley, they have to be even deprived of their right to live in other parts of their home state.

Such narrow-mindedness and parochial thinking violates the letter and spirit of our Constitution and hurts the moral content and ethos of our nationhood. It is worth recalling here that during the Maharaja's rule thousands of Dogras had been granted *jagirs* in the Valley and had been living happily there on a permanent basis.

The children of KP migrants faced another very serious problem — that of admissions in local schools and colleges. For a community with high levels of education and literacy and traditional preference for professional and whitecollar jobs, the education of children is a subject of topmost priority and concern. So when the KP children came to Jammu after the Exodus and later, they suffered the trauma of losing their friends and classmates, and the good quality schools which many of them had been attending. Their admission to government schools was opposed by the local people at Jammu. Eventually parallel sections and additional shifts in these schools were arranged for the migrant children. Initially some makeshift schools were also opened within the migrant camps for primary level children. These schools were opened in tents, which often lacked basic equipment like blackboards and chalk Besides, in the terrible heat of Jammu summer (temperature 40 °-45°), there were no fans and in the rains the tents were flooded. There was no drinking water readily available and no toilets. Little children sometimes fainted because of the heat, exhaustion and dehydration. But poor things they slogged on nevertheless aware and conscious of the anxieties of the parents regarding their education. Things are much better now and little girls and boys can be seen going smartly about in their school uniforms attending normal schools.

Lots of well-qualified young women would love to work in schools to provide good quality education to children and also to augment the family incomes. But they are not getting any jobs in the government schools. Some of them have been working in private schools but in many such schools they are underpaid.

It is well-known that in difficult circumstances women show more resistance and resourcefulness in managing troublesome matters. But at the same time they are much more sensitive to nuances of human behaviour, ambience of a place, the needs of children and family and overall atmosphere of a place called home. They are thus more open to stress. In our samples of migrant population almost half the women reported suffering from anxiety (for no immediate reason)/mental tension/bouts of depression/blood pressure/headaches and body pains and even skin rashes. They have also fallen prey to serious ailments or there has been aggravation of already existing ailments like diabetes, heart disease, ulcers, kidney problems, and even cancer caused by prolonged state of tension and stress. Women have also been much concerned and saddened by the social and cultural implications of the migration. There has been widespread break-up of joint/extended families and weakening/dilution of cultural traditions, customs and celebration of festivals, both social and religious. For some it has been very painful to celebrate their daughters' marriages in the most ordinary manner with ordinary families, a far cry from their earlier conditions. Another sad thing for the women has been the loss of old neighbourhoods and good neighbourly relationships, especially during major events like marriages etc., or difficult situations like a death in the family.

There is the case of a migrant family (S. No. 223) living in rented rooms at Jammu. The mother of the informant had died. Their landlord insisted that the dead body be taken out of the house immediately. It took them about five hours to make the required preparations for the funeral and get hold of a priest to perform the rituals and take the body for cremation. All this time the body had to be kept by the roadside. In moments of exasperation, they have sometimes, given in to feelings of despair, "It is better to die in Kashmir than to face all these problems at Jammu," a lady once remarked (S. No. 18).

The students studying in the medical and engineering colleges in Kashmir after leaving the Valley were instructed to report at various colleges in other states of India and pursue their studies there under special arrangements made by the governments. In the process, some students lost a year or more. Some felt much disturbed over the attendant uncertainty and degree of mental and physical effort needed to adjust to social and academic ambience of the new institutions. "Some of my classmates," says a doctor (S. No. 504) "took to alcohol during this phase." He had been a first year MBBS student at Srinagar medical college but had to shift to a medical college in Himachal Pradesh.

There is among the members of the community widespread appreciation and deep gratitude for the Maharashtra government, which came to the rescue of the aspiring young boys and girls of the community by offering reservation of seats in the professional colleges in the state soon after the Exodus. This facility has remained available since, in spite of the changes in government through elections and irrespective of the political parties in power. Hundreds have also benefitted from the reservation of seats made in all engineering, management and planning institutions by the Ministry of Human Resources Development, Govt, of India since the year 2000.

There has been a silver lining to the dark clouds of human tragedy consequent upon the uprooting of the community; the children and the youth have been exposed to a much wider world - outside the Valley — and have gained much richer experience of life from an early stage in their lives. Some of them have been able to pursue professional courses that they might not have even heard of while in Kashmir. This experience has also given them the impetus to think bigger and higher in terms of the threshold of their ambition in life. After all a scattered community lacking the force of numbers in such a huge democratic polity as that of India, but with the Brahmanic tradition of deep commitment to pursuit of knowledge and learning, has only one option to maintain its identity and serve the community, the country and humanity at large and that is, to pursue excellence in all areas of intellectual endeavour. That is the path to true empowerment of the community. Here are two quotes from two women migrants:

(a) **S. No. 363** "We miss our home, land, neighbours, friends and people. Now we are settled here but life lacks charm."

(b) **S. No. 446** "An uprooted tree may be transplanted and it may grow and survive but not the same way as before. There is bound to be some change."

(c) And from 16 year old Sakshi (**S. No. 426**) "I was 3 years old in 1989 when my family migrated to Delhi. I grew up here, attended my school here, and am happy with my friends here. About Kashmir I do not know anything worth mentioning."

Finally a charming little story, most probably true, that we heard at Jammu. A migrant woman one day, by chance met a Muslim neighbour from her village in Kashmir, in the market place at Jammu. After exchanging greetings the woman enquired about the happenings in Kashmir and the people of her village. Then she casually asked, "And what is the latest about your 'Azadi?' The Muslim neighbour mumbled a vague reply. "Well, dear brother," the lady commented, "I do not know about your 'Azadi' but, believe me, we have achieved it here."

Table I (Part 1)
Particulars of Kashmiri Pandit Women Killed By Terrorists

Source: M. L. Raina (ed) "Kashmir Documents'* 2004; P.77-94, 1,313-315				
Sl. No.	*Name*	*Occupation*	*Date*	*Place*
1.	Mrs. Sheela Tikoo	Housewife	1.11.1989	Srinagar
2.	Mrs. Devi	Housewife	March 1990	Housewife
3.	Mrs. Sarla Bhat	Service	25.4.90	Anantnag
4.	Mrs. Prana Ganjoo	Service	07.05.90	Sopore
5.	Dolly	Service	07.05.90	Srinagar
6.	Hindu woman kidnapped and killed	Govt. Employee	30.5.90	Srinagar
7.	Mrs. Durga Kaul (Plus her husband Badri Kaul)	Housewife	18.06.90	Srinagar
8.	Mrs. Prana Ganjoo	Housewife	18.06.90	Srinagar
9.	K. P. young woman (and Brijnath Kaul, her husband) tied to a vehicle and dragged to death	Housewife	26.06.90	Anantnag (had come from Shopian)
10.	Babli (plus mother, No. 11)	Student	01.07.90	Pulwama
11.	Mrs. Roopwati (plus daughter, No. 10)	Housewife	01,07.90	Pulwama
12.	Mrs. Tej Dhar (plus husband & daughter No. 13)	Housewife	01.07.90	Srinagar
13.	Girija Dhar (d/o 12)	Housewife	01.07.90	Srinagar
14.	Mrs. Arundhati	Housewife	02.07.90	Srinagar
15.	Mrs. Sahni	Doctor	18.07.90	Anantnag
16	Mrs. Baljeet Kaur		17.08.90	Sopore
17	Mrs. Usha ji		14.10.90	Srinagar
18.	Mrs. Neetaji		14.10.90	Srinagar
19.	Mrs. Nirmala Raina	Housewife	6.3.2000	Anantnag

Table I (Part 2)
Particulars of Kashmiri Pandit Women Killed By Terrorists
Wandahama Massacre 26.01.1998

20	Smt Choti		25	Smt Shadilal
21	Smt Asha ji		26	Smt. Dulari
22	Ms. Sarika		27	Ms. Vijay Kumari
23	Ms. Neema		28	Ms. Seema
24	Ms. Jyoti		29	Ms. Meenakshi

Nadimarg Massacre : 23.03.2003

30	Mrs. Ashaji (Husband, son and daughters)	Housewife		36	Ms. Princy (Govt. Employee)
31	Ms. Girija			37	Ms. Sushma Govt. Employee (Father & brother)
32	Mrs. Rekha ji (2 year old baby & father-in-law)	Housewife		38	Mrs. Suman ji, Housewife (2 year baby)
11	Ms. Rajni (father)	Student		39	Mrs. Devaki, Housewife (Son & Grandson)
33	Mrs. Chand Rani	Housewife		40	Mrs. Geeta ji, Housewife (Daughter, husband, son & Brother-in-law)
35	Ms. Preetma (d/o 38)				

CHAPTER – 9

NADIMARG MASSACRE - THE FULL STORY

Nadimarg has been a biggish prosperous looking village in South Kashmir Valley, like many such around that area. This village has the distinction of belonging to two tehsils Kulgam and Shopian, and thereby two districts, namely Anantnag and Pulwama. The borderline is a stream running through the village.

March 23, 2003 was a normal sunny and peaceful day. This was the day when Australia-India World Cup cricket final was being played in Australia. Like elsewhere in India, here too, people had been watching the game on their television sets.

Around 10.30 PM, when the villagers had retired for supper and night's rest, there was sudden commotion and disturbance in the area where the Hindus lived. A group of masked men carrying arms and wearing army uniforms had descended on the village and shattered the peaceful hour and the ambience. They shouted loudly for all Hindu families (adults and children) to come out of their homes and line up in the open area. They assured them that they were army jawans and there was nothing to be afiaid of. They had come over for a 'crackdown' (cordon and search operation), as some militants were suspected to be hiding around the locality. They were speaking in Hindustani. As members of the eight Hindu

(Kashmiri Pandit) families obeyed the instructions and lined up in the open - men, women and children - they were shot down at point blank range. In all, 24 people were killed; only a few people could escape alive partly by luck and partly by pluck. The terrorists left the village after the carnage. They were there for barely half an hour. The family-wise description of the episode and their experience is given below: Also see the Table listing the people killed in the massacre, with some relevant information based on our survey data.

In all, nine Kashmiri Pandit families were staying in the village at that time.

1. **Family of Jagar Nath: (retired government employee):** Jagar Nath and his wife Shanti had at the time gone to Jammu. His son Bhushan Lal (28) hid himself on a walnut tree. His wife Pamposh (27) picked up her two kids Arti (5) and Ramesh (1) and took shelter under a storehouse (built a little above the ground). While these people were running away to hide somewhere their uncle (Jagar Nath's brother) diverted the attention of the terrorists by loud shouts. He himself could not run fast, as one of his leg's had been amputated some years back following a road accident. The terrorists shot at him and left him wounded. He was later carried home, but died the same night due to heavy loss of blood.
2. **Family of Bansi Lal; (government employee):** Theirs was one of the most prosperous families in the village with three working people together earning Rs. 21,000/- as monthly salary. They had besides, agricultural land, etc. Bansi Lals wife, Asha Ji was an educated, good looking and remarkably smart and social lady with leadership qualities. She had the

ability and the confidence to be able to interact with government officials, BSF officers, police personnel and political leaders in the area and even militants suspected to be visiting the village in the disguise (by pretending to be well wishers of the Hindus as fellow Kashmiris) of some kind of "voluntary workers" to maintain peace in the area in the face of prevalent violence in the Valley. This lady was killed along with her husband, son Rakesh (19) a student and two daughters Princy (27) and Girija (28). The only surviving member of the family is the elder son Vijay (30) who had gone to Jammu to meet his fiancee's and mother's families.

Asha Ji is reported to have even rebuked the terrorists roundly before being gunned down to silence.

3. **Family of Mohan Lal Bhat (retired government employee):** A widower; he was killed along with his son Pradiman Krishna (29) and daughter Sushma (27). He was elder brother of Bansi Lal (Family No. 1) No survivors.

4. **Family of Triloki Nath Bhat (teacher):** He himself was killed. But his wife Sheela (50) managed to get hold of her 3 month old grandson Baby and hide in a safe corner. Her daughter-in-law Rita (28) picked up her sons Rohit (5) and Akshay (3) and ran away. Her husband Ramesh (30) had quietly slipped away by a circuitous route to alert the policemen at Zainpora police station and seek help. He was detained there for the night but no action was taken by the policemen present. Thus Sheela, her 3. month-old grandson Baby, her son Ramesh, his wife Rita, and

their two kids escaped death. Sheela's unmarried daughter Jyoti *(26)* an arts graduate, jumped out and climbed the walnut tree behind their house and hid there. She too was saved. But Sheela's two daughters-in-law Rekha (30) and Suman (25) along with their two babies Suraj (2) and Manish (2) respectively, held in their arms, were shot dead. Sheela's other two sons (a) Manohar Lal (32) who was at Jammu and (b) Satish (28) who was elsewhere survived. Satish's 3-month-old baby is now being taken care of by his grandmother (Sheela) and aunt Jyoti.

5. **Family of Bansi Lal Bhat (retired government employee):** His 80 year old mother Devaki was bed-ridden. She was left alone. His wife Phoolaji (58) went out to a safe hiding place and their son Chand ji (24) hid himself in the chimney of the cooking fireplace *(choolha).* The elder son Shabji (33) and his wife Jeetaji (30) and their baby (3) had already migrated to Jammu.

   The terrorists dragged out Bansi Lal from his house. His daughter Ranjini (28) a B. A. student tried to shield him and asked for mercy. Both were shot dead.

6. **Family of Avtar Krishen (village pradhan):** His wife Usha (40), son Ramesh (20), a policeman, and daughter Nisha (23) were away at Pulwama. But he himself, his mother Devaki (65) and younger son Amit were at home, all three were killed.

7. **Family of Chooni Lal Kaul (electrician):** He has been a very popular person in the area by virtue of his good conduct and kind and helpful nature. He and his wife were both shot at and his wife, Chand

Rani (58) died. He received a bullet in his leg, fell down and pretended death, and survived. He had already lost one arm in an accident during his work as foreman in the electricity department His two sons Kakaji (24) and Deepji (22) and daughter Rajni (20) escaped death, as they were away.

8. **Family of Radha Krishen (retired employee):** He himself, his wife Gita Ji (50) and daughter Preetma (25) and his brother Loke Nath (55) on a visit from Jammu where he had shifted in 1994 were all killed. Mohan Lal (20) son of Radha Krishen somehow managed to escape to safety by hiding. Loke Nath is survived by his wife Bimla (35) and daughters Neeru (12) and Anu (7). They were at Jammu.
9. **Family of Somnath (retired government employee):** His family consists of wife, Shama (50), three sons Kamal Ji (32) and Deep Ji (28) and Manohar Nath (35) a policeman, his wife Anita, (28) and son Anil (1). Only parents and one son were there on that fateful night. Having sensed the danger they ran away quietly and took shelter in some house away from the village. They were all saved. This was the only family, which had no casualty at all. They stayed on in the village for about eight months after the carnage and finally shifted to Jammu.

Background and Aftermath

These Kashmiri Pandit families had been staying in the village Nadimarg all these years after the exodus of 1990 in spite of all odds. The relations with their Muslim neighbours in the village and also those in the neighbouring villages had been good and friendly. Quite a few members of these families were either pensioners or working as junior level employees in various government departments. Besides, each family had some agricultural lands and orchards. By sheer hard work and small investments on their lands over the years they had been able to generate good returns from their lands. Each household also had milch cows and oxen for agricultural purposes. There was a well-maintained temple in the village for daily visits and for celebration of special occasions. Things were quite peaceful and life went on at a normal pace even in the context of occasional trouble in the Valley and some incidents in the adjoining areas.

For general security, a BSF company had been stationed there for several years but it had been withdrawn some time back. It had been replaced by a police post in the village. But strangely on the day of the carnage most of the policemen were on leave. The remaining policemen meekly surrendered to the terrorists letting them take away their arms and also the wireless set. There has been some suspicion among the victims that most probably the policemen had prior knowledge of the events to follow. They did not even exhibit any pretence of resistance to the terrorists and their actions.

A delegation of the Hindu residents had a couple of weeks earlier met the Deputy Commissioner, Anantnag district about some rumours they had heard about possible trouble in their area from the terrorists. The lady IAS officer had not taken their plea seriously saying if nothing adverse had happened all these years there could not be any danger now. Within weeks of this meeting, the carnage had proved her wrong, terribly wrong.

The carnage, when it actually happened, received worldwide publicity, and messages of sympathy were received even from various foreign governments including the Pakistan government.

Possible Reasons

In course of the author's detailed interviews with the residents and the victims of the massacre at Nadimarg, at Jammu, one could not pinpoint any possible provocation for the killings. They could only make some guesses:

(a) Since the KP families gave the impression of being happy and prosperous by the way they had improved the quality, size and the look of their homes, and the way they celebrated their festivals and weddings etc. this might have aroused feelings of envy and jealousy in some quarters.

(b) The *bon-homie* enjoyed by the KP residents with officers and men of the BSF, who would gladly participate in the religious ceremonies being organised at the village temple, might have angered the militants.

(c) Some people reported that some Kashmiri Muslims would also occasionally visit the village and KP homes in the guise of "well wishers and peacekeepers" and accept their hospitality for short durations and then go away quietly. Possibly they were disguised militants or/and their agents paying occasional visits to feel the pulse of the situation and gather useful intelligence. Even the local policemen and their officers were received cordially by the villagers on their visits.

(d) This complex interplay and overlap of overt friendly relationships with government officials, BSF personnel, police officers and men, local petty politicians, and friendly local "peacekeepers" etc. could have rubbed some people the wrongly way. The upshot could only be trouble.

(e) Finally it has to be accepted that the militants/terrorists do not need any special reason or provocation, real or imagined for committing violence and atrocities against the targeted people.

Be that as it may, the after-effects of the massacre caused a lot of ripples all over the Indian subcontinent and beyond, as it attracted high voltage publicity on television, radio, and the print media. L. K. Advani, then Deputy Prime Minister and Home Minister of India, visited Nadimarg the very next day. He met a group of angry surviving Kashmiri Pandits who kept asking questions and seeking answers regarding this tragic event One young man, Ramesh who was greatly agitated (five members of his family had been killed) went up to him pushing aside the security men, put his hands on his shoulders and asked why such a thing had to happen. He felt crazy with pain and anguish and his eyes asked a million questions to which nobody had any answers. The security people took him aside and tried to calm him down with many assurances of help and future protection.

Mufti Mohammad Sayeed, Chief Minister of Jammu and Kashmir and his daughter Mehbooba Sayeed also came, promised lot of help and advised the survivors to stay on in the village in spite of what had happened. In fact Mehbooba stayed on in the village for a whole week till the last rites were performed. Sonia Gandhi, Congress president also came to the village to convey sympathy and support. The representatives of many NGOs also came with help and sympathy. An army of media people swarmed to this place to cover the story in painful detail with heart-rending visuals. One of the most pleasant parts of the story was the concern and sympathy shown by the local Muslim population by large-scale participation in the mourning for the Hindus killed in the massacre. Were any of the terrorists involved also in the crowd? Who knows?

Some families stayed on at Nadimarg for some time, but ultimately all of them shifted to Jammu. The Government of India and the Jammu and Kashmir state government paid compensation to all the affected families as per the assurance given. However, during our investigation we noticed general reluctance among the families of the victims, to talk about this episode as it aroused extremely painful memories in their minds.

This description of Nadimarg incident shows in graphic detail the nature and character of the mindless hostility shown by the terrorists, and their sponsors and supporters, towards the Kashmiri Pandit minority in the Kashmir Valley.

Table I

Massacre at Nadimarg Kashmir Valley: March 23,2003

Particulars of Persons Killed

S l . No.	*Head of Household*	*Sl. no.*	*Persons Killed*	*Age*	*Sex*	*Education*	*Occupation Income*
1.	Jagar Nath	1	Lassa Kak	60	M	Class 8	Retired govt. employee (Rs. 1800)
II.	Bansi Lal	2	Bansi Lal	50	M	Class 10	Govt. employee (Rs. 10,000)
		3	Mrs. Asha ji (wife of 2)	48	F	Class 5	Housewife
		4	Rakesh (S/o 2 & 3)	19	M	T.D.C.	Student
		5	Ms. Princy (D/o 2 & 3)	27	F	T.D.C.	Govt. employee (Rs. 5000)
		6	Ms. Girija Kumari (S/o 2 & 3)	28	F	Class 5	
III.	Mohanlal Bhat	7	Mohan Lal	62	M	Class 8	Retd. Govt. employee (Rs. 1800)
		8	Ms. Sushma	27	F	T.D.C.	Part Time Govt. employee (Rs. 800)
		9	Pradiman Krishna (S/o 7)	29	M	Class 10	
IV.	Triloki Nath	10	Triloki Nath	55	M	Class 8	Teacher (Rs. 5,000)
		11	Mrs. Rekha ji (Ruby) (Daughter -in-law of 10)	30	F	Class 10	Housewife
		12	Baby Suraj(S/o 11)	2	M		
		13	Mrs. Suman ji (Julie: D-in-law of 10)	25	F	Class 10	Housewife
		14	Baby Manish (Monu; S/o 13)	2	M		
V.	Bansi Lal Bhat	15	Bansi Lal	63	M	Class 8	Retd. Govt. employee (Rs. 3000)
		16	Ms. Rajni D/o 15	28	F	B.A. I[st] Year	Student

VI.	Avtar Krishna	17	Mrs Avtar Krishna	38	M	Class 8	Village Pradhan (Rs. 300)
		18	Mrs. Devaki (M/o 17)	65	F		Housewife
		19	Am it Kumar (S/o 17)	17	M	P.U.C.	Student
VII.	Chooni Lal Kaul	20	Mrs. Chand Rani (W/o head)	58	F		Housewife
VIII.	Radha Krishna	21	Radha Krishna	63	M	Class 8	Retd. Govt. employee (Rs. 1500)
		22	Mrs. Geeta Ji (W/o 21)	50	F		Housewife
		23	Ms. Preetma (D/o 21 & 22)	25	F	T.D.C.	
		24	Lok Nath (B/o 21)	55	M	Class 8	Govt. employee (Rs.4500)

Total No. of persons killed = 24 [Males-13(thirteen) Females = 11 (eleven)]

This includes two male babies aged barely two years each. They were shot dead along with their mothers. (The detailed data in this table were collected during our survey conducted in village Nadimarg in December 2002,about four months before the tragic event. The supplementary data were collected by the author during interviews with some surviving members of the affected families in April- May 2004 at Jammu)

CHAPTER – 10

RANDOM CASES: SOME CONCISE STATEMENTS

Herein are given some concise statements culled from the recorded interviews with our informants chosen at random. The statements convey the views of the Kashmiri Pandit migrants on various matters of their concern. These are reproduced here without any comment, as their import and implications are self-evident and very meaningful.

The heading in each case here indicates the serial number and the code number of the concerned schedule (questionnaire) and the place of origin and the location of the camp of the migrant interviewed. No names are mentioned to protect the identity of the interviewees.

1. S. No. 27 JC - 81,304; Vessu, Anantnag; Udhampur

Reasons for migration

-> Killing of prominent Hindu people by militants spread fear in the Hindu community, fled for life.

Problems faced after migration:

-> Son's education suffered.

-> Financial problems - money and ration provided by government not sufficient.

-> Post-migration anxiety and tension led to husband's illness and untimely death.

–> Health of community suffered.

Suggestions

–> The whole world should come together and form an army to fight militancy and terrorism across the world.

2. S. No. 274; JC, D - 5; 345; Srinagar; Delhi

Comments

–> Never want to go back to Kashmir as it has snatched everything from them.

3. S. No. 275; JC; D - 6; 346; Chhanapora/ Anantnag; Delhi

–> Grudges:

Angry at the insurance system as whole insurance money was not given.

Current state of mind:

–> Want to go back to the Valley, but are aware that they will not be accepted as residents.

4. S. No. 277; JC; D — 9; 349; Anantnag; Delhi

Effects

–> Education of son affected; lost motivation and interest in further studies.

Views on going back

–> Do not want to go back to the Valley ever.

5. S. No. 300; JC; D —10; 350; Baramula; Delhi

Effects

–> Business was affected, great loss.

–> Sold land and house.

–> Migration caused division among brothers.

6. S. No. 271; JC; D - 12; 352; Bandipora; Delhi

State of mind

–> Optimistic

Reasons for not selling property:

–> Want to go back and settle.

–> So far, no profitable deal.

Views:

–> Believe in inter-caste marriage.

7. S. No. 272; JC; D -14; 354; Habakadal; Srinagar Delhi

Reasons for migration:

–> Initially in 1989, did not migrate thinking they could withstand disturbances, but left immediately when militants threatened to kill baby daughter.

8. S. No. 255; CC; D -16; 356; Budgam District; Delhi

Reasons for migration:

–> Family members killed by militants.

9. S. No. 205; CC; D-17; 357; Gandhar Pora; Delhi -

Reasons for migrating

–> General terror.

–> Had to get help for rations, utensils etc. from relatives living in foreign countries.

On going back to the Valley:

–> Shall go back when the situation is such that the Chief Minister is able to walk without his armed escort.

10. S. No. 201; CC; D -18; 358; Ranipora; Anantnag; Delhi

Reasons for migration:

–> Heightened terror and killing of prominent Hindus.

Effects of migration (as stated):

–> Informant's graduation got delayed.

–> Loss of property and work.

–> Dislocation, so very painful.

11. S. No. 222; CC; D - 19; 359; Anantnag; Delhi

Effects of migration:

–> Wife died, could not bear Delhi's heat

On going back:

–> Have not sold house as they think if in future conditions improve they could go back to the Valley and at least have a place to stay.

12. S. N. 236; CC; D-21; 361; Baramula; Delhi-

Effects of migration:

–> Lost every thing - did not have a single penny or piece of land.

–> Head of family died on the way from Kashmir to Delhi due to enormous shock.

13. S. N. 72; M. App; D-26; 366; Sonwarah;Srinagar; Delhi

Reasons of migration:

–> Threatening calls and notes.

–> Listed in militants' list.

–> Killing of neighbour's family.

–> Many females in the family.

Property:

–> Their houses occupied by militants.

On going back:

–> Parents do not expect in their lifetime a situation conducive enough for them to go back.

–> Children do not want to go back due to lack of future prospects.

14. S. No. 41; M. App; D - 28: 368; Chanpura; Delhi —

Reasons for migration:

–> Threatening letter to husband.

On going back:

–> Do not want to go back, no future.

15. S. No. 254; Mahagon Estates; D - 43; 383; Shivpura; Delhi

Effects of migration:

–> Studies of children affected.

–> Health - skin disease.

–> Son was emotionally disturbed.

Impression of State and Central governments:

–> Hindustan 'looto.'

–> Islamization of Kashmir.

On going back:

–> Want to go back.

16. S. No. 256; D - 47; Mahagon Estates; 387; Nawgam Bypass; Delhi

Reasons for migration:

–> Informant's father killed by militants.

Effects of migration:

–> Informant's wife was pregnant during migration, lost child by miscarriage.

17. S. No. 259; D - 50; 390; Verinag; Anantnag; Kashmiri Colony; Delhi

Reasons for migration:

–> Situation grim.

–> To save women and children.

Effects of migration:

–> Loss of house and goods.

–> Health problems.

–> Financial strain.

Present state of mind:

–> Positive.

Present condition:

–> Family is well placed and comfortably settled; look towards a bright future.

18. S. No. 104; D-53; 392; Srinagar; Kashmiri Colony; Delhi

Reasons for migrating:

–> Terror, fear for life.

Effects of migration:

–> Loss of home and property.

–> Father died due to mental stress leading to hypertension.

–> Unsuitable weather.

–> Financial strain.

–> Pathetic life.

19. S. No. 196; D - 56; 395; Sai Sadak; Kashmiri Colony; Delhi

Reasons for migrating:

–> Atmosphere not safe for living.

–> A friend was killed by militants.

–> Threatening calls by militants.

–> Safety of women and children.

Effects of migration:

–> Loss of house, property.

–> Initially had to stay in camps, women and girls had no privacy.

–> No financial support from government. No insurance.

–> Health problems due to hot weather and pollution.

–> Head of family became heart patient. Underwent bypass surgery, no medical allowance from government.

20. S. No. 287; D - 61; 400; Anantnag; Kashmiri Colony; Delhi

Effects of migration:

–> Informant's mother-in-law died of depression.

-> Consequently father-in-law fell ill, later regained health.

21. S. No. 14; D-64; 403; Safakadal; Srinagar; Kashmiri Colony; Delhi

Effects of migration:

Negative:

-> Elder family members died due to depression and skin cancer.

Positive:

-> Migration has given Kashmiri Pandits more exposure and opportunities.

-> Better career opportunities.

On going back:

-> Want to see their home, not to settle down.

22. S. No. 39 D - 66; 405; Anantnag; Kashmiri Colony; Delhi

Reasons for migration:

-> Business was attacked by militants.

-> Threat to life.

Effects of migration:

-> Excessive financial problems, had to struggle a lot initially for survival.

Current status:

-> Son has established own business.

-> Daughter and son are married to Kashmiri Pandits.

23. S. No. 8; D - 68; Zanipur; Pulwama; Kashmiri Colony; Delhi

Reasons for migration:

–> Bomb blast at home by militants, 5 family members injured no proper treatment in government hospitals.

–> Also, uncle in defence so militancy threat.

–> Women under threat - militants threatened to convert them as Muslims and take them to Pakistan.

Fight for right (after migration):

–> Helped a lot by Kashmiri Samiti.

–> Participated in rallies.

Problems faced (after migration):

–> Life in community hall miserable. 28 families inside hall.

–> A senior family member died of cancer, no money for advanced treatments.

–> Daughter had a paralytic attack. Son fell ill with meningitis — still under treatment

24. S. No. 1; D - 69; Anantnag; Kashmiri Colony; Delhi -

Reasons for migration:

–> Close friend was shot dead.

–> Constant threat to life.

–> The honour of women and girls was at stake.

Education:

–> Children completed their education in Jammu.

Current status:

–> Daughter married to Kashmiri Pandit in Delhi.

–> Son working in Delhi.

25. S. No. 2; D - 70; 409; Fatehkadal; Srinagar; Kashmiri Colony; Delhi

<u>Reasons for migration:</u>

–> Militants threatened to kill brother who is in the army.

–> Other family members also threatened.

<u>Family in Kashmir:</u>

–> One brother who is in the army with family.

–> Came to Delhi for vacation. On return had narrow escape from bomb blast in the car in which they travelled.

<u>Noteworthy incident:</u>

–> During mother's journey to Srinagar to see son "Area Commander” of militants took care of her.

<u>Problems faced after migration:</u>

–> Initially one rented room for seven members, lot of difficulties.

–> Father died due to hypertension and diabetes.

<u>On going back</u>

–> Children miss their home and want to go back to their homeland.

26. S. No. 3; D - 71; 410; Kokarnag; Anantnag; Kashmiri Colony; Delhi

<u>Reason for migration:</u>

–> Neighbour's (a) Head of family was brutally murdered, badly tortured and hung, and his son was also killed.

–> Girl's body was chopped.

–> A boy's tongue was cut.

Migration:

–> Migrated with four families in a truck and took nothing along with them.

–> Thought they would return. First migrated to Jammu, later to Delhi.

Problems after migration:

–> Initially in tents in Jammu, pathetic condition.

–> Then many families together in rented rooms causing social and psychological problems to girls and women.

–> People from joint families felt separation, trauma, and social uprootedness.

–> Health problems duc to hot weather.

–> Children not admitted to good schools.

27. S. No. 4; D - 72; 411; Srinagar; Kashmiri Colony; Delhi -

Reasons for migration:

–> House was burnt, as it was adjacent to temple.

–> Militants threatened to kill.

–> Militants demanded surrender of children around 15 years of age.

–> One CID inspector was killed by militants. Being a CID informant was more vulnerable

–> Informant also in private job, expelled by Muslims.

Current status:

–> Family in Delhi, son works here.

–> Daughters married to Kashmiri Pandits in Delhi and in Panipat.

Effects of migration:

–> An elder family member died, as food and weather conditions did not suit

28. S. N. 5; D - 73; 412; Harwan, Srinagar; Kashmiri Colony; Delhi

Reasons for migration:

–> Political turmoil, communal tensions.

–> Killing of central/state government employees.

–> A known teacher was killed by his students.

Problems faced during and after migration:

–> During migration informant's wife pregnant.

–> No adequate medical care/facilities. Consequently at birth, daughter infected with septicaemia; at 2 years diagnosed with epilepsy, under treatment

–> Deaths due to snake bites, epidemics.

–> Mental/psychological blocks in children's minds.

–> Human rights violation—no steps taken by government.

Complaints:

–> On visiting Srinagar they found that BSF and Army personnel were living in their houses.

–> Government had not taken any property under its control or security.

–> No steps by the government for permanent rehabilitation.

29. S. No. 21; D – 76; 415; Habakadal; Srinagar; Kashmiri Colony; Delhi

Reasons for migration:

-> Militants burnt their houses.

-> BJP leader, who lived in the same street, was killed.

Effects of migration:

-> Informant's father-in-law died of heart attack, mother-in-law suffering from hypertension.

-> Faced many problems after migration.

Present state of mind:

-> Still miss the big house and the life, which they had back home.

30. S. No. 219; D- 80; 419; Anantnag; Kashmir; Kashmiri Colony; Delhi

Reasons stated for migration:

-> Business establishment was destroyed.

Effects of migration:

-> Initially had to stay in relief migrant camps where conditions were pathetic.

-> Education affected.

-> Birth rate of Kashmiris gone down to 10%.

-> Death rate gone up to 35%.

-> 90% of elders are diabetics.

-> Informant's mother died due to a heart attack.

Views:

-> Kashmiri migrants are like animals in a zoo - people talk to them, make films on them, make false promises, do nothing.

-> There is no synchronisation between the declared government policies and the actual execution of these policies.

31. S. No 224; D - 89; 428; Verinag; Anantnag; Kashmiri Colony; Delhi

Reasons for migration:

–> Informant's father's cousin was shot dead.

Informant's state of mind:

–> Worried and sceptical about providing information related to his and his father's job and his family's problems in general.

CHAPTER – 11

RELIEF AND REHABILITATION

The uprooted Kashmiri Pandits are officially and otherwise referred to as 'migrants'. Many leaders and members of the community think it is a misnomer as the term implies voluntary movement, which is not the case here. They would prefer to call themselves as "Internally Displaced Persons (IDP)", which description is certainly close to reality. The mass exodus of Kashmiri Pandits in 1989-90 from Kashmir Valley, as is well known and well established, happened in an atmosphere of violent acts and threats of further violence against them from the terrorist and militant outfits operating in the Valley. Neither the civil administration nor the security forces of the state and central governments were in a position to offer them suitable protection from the sporadic violence and target killings directed against them across the Valley. Now (2005) fifteen years have passed since this unfortunate event and KPs continue to live outside the Valley many of them still in camps.

In the first flush of the event in early 1990 when hordes of KP families started pouring into Jammu across the Banihal tunnel, the then Governor of Jammu and Kashmir State, Jagmohan (the State being then under Governor's rule) announced a series of emergency relief measures for them. These were -

1. **Accommodation:** It was initially arranged in tents, which were erected in available open spaces at Jammu,

Udhampur, Nagrota etc. These became regular "migrant" camps and soon work started on providing the basic facilities like water, electricity, roads and pathways etc. In Delhi and other places community halls and other such available spaces were utilized for the purpose.

2. **Rations:** Identity cards were issued to all registered migrant families/individuals to enable them to draw free rations at the following rates -

   (A) Rice: - 9 kilogram per head per month

   (B) Flour (Wheat): - 2 kilogram per head per month.

   (C) Sugar: - 1 kilogram per family per month at a flat rate.

3. **Cash Allowance:** Each family of four or more members could claim a cash allowance of Rs. 2400/- per month for overhead expenses. The families with only three or lesser members received cash allowance at Rs. 600/- per head.

   This allowance amount has since the year 2004 been increased to Rs. 3000/- per month. Any pensioner could claim cash compensation only to the extent his/her pension fell short of the entitled cash allowance amount.

4. **Medical Dispensary:** In due course each major camp was provided with a medical dispensary to serve as a basic medical facility for camp residents.

5. **Basic School:** Some basic/primary schools were also opened near major migrant camps for the children's sake.

6. **Salary for Government Employees:** While some permanent government employees among the migrant KPs were able to join respective posts of duty in Jammu many others could not do so for lack of suitable vacancies or because they had migrated to places outside the Jammu

and Kashmir State. Such employees were allowed to draw their normal salaries (and pension as and when due) till their entitled tenure of service as if they had been all along on duty. Only in such cases no promotions to higher posts were allowed.

This was a major concession but the number of persons enjoying this benefit has not been large. When members of a community are forced to abandon their homes suddenly and have to flea for dear life their immediate concern is survival — physical survival - as other things could be taken care of only when conditions become more stable. The relief package announced and executed under orders of the Governor of Jammu and Kashmir state in early 1990 came like manna from heaven to the harassed and harried KPs. This package saved lives and was a morale booster to the demoralized community caught in a whirlpool of confusion and chaos.

Not that the conditions were and have been altogether satisfactory - far from that. Any relief measures cannot be too good because they are not a product of any well thought out planning and forethought but only a quick response to an unforeseen and sudden development of a destructive nature whether caused by natural forces or human follies.

First of all the barren areas available/chosen for establishing migrant camps were away from or on the fringes of the concerned cities and towns entirely lacking in basic amenities for human habitation. Some places were infested with poisonous snakes and scorpions and these creatures had an easy entry into the tents as a cooler shelter in the scorching heat of a Jammu summer. Quite a few casualties - some fatal - were caused by them. Scarcity of water and electricity and lack of electric fans were a major problem for a long time. Even little children attending the ill equipped camp schools stoically faced the problem of lack of black-boards, drinking water, toilets and fans in these schools in the initial phase.

The tents provided to families were one-room shelters with no kitchen and toilet spaces marked out, and no privacy worth the name for women- folk/married couples/old people/ children.

The medical facilities in the dispensaries were very nominal in the beginning and people had to go all the way to the crowded government hospitals or to private practitioners for any persistent health problems. They could ill afford to spend long hours and money on these visits.

After some years the tents were replaced with one-room *pucca* apartments - one for each family. But again there were no spaces for kitchen, toilet and bath attached to these. This was a serious shortcoming. Some common toilet facilities were provided in camps, which were far from satisfactory or adequate in terms of needs of the residents. The maintenance work of these buildings is done by private contractors and they do not usually do a good job of it because of corrupt practices.

The Prime Minister of India, Manmohan Singh ordered, after a visit to the migrant camps in 2004, that the one-room apartments be replaced with improved two-room apartments in all the camps. This decision has been in answer to a long-standing demand of the migrants and has come as a great relief to the community. A two-room flat can offer some privacy to the family members. The "migrant camp" settlements are now vastly improved habitations compared to what they were to begin with. The basic amenities like water, electricity, roads, adequate transport, good schools and better medical dispensaries and shops for essential daily supplies (vegetables, groceries, milk, medicine etc.) have since come up close to the camps. Even small temples have been built in the camp areas (by the residents from their own resources) to meet their spiritual and religious needs. Several small shops within the camp areas are being run by some of the enterprising residents themselves as a measure of self-help and community service. Also relief measures from the government are being extended to the registered migrants as per orders with due regularity.

Since there is not much hope of an early return to their homes and properties in Kashmir Valley there is stoic acceptance of the prevailing state of affairs and life in exile. Obviously these camps are now homes away from home. Around these temporary and ad-hoc settlements neighbourhood relationships and community life have grown in an adequate measure. There may be mutual jealousies sometimes but a spirit of mutual cooperation and self-help is in the air. Some of the young men and women — who were just little children in 1989- 90 have had the opportunity of higher/professional education and are now employed in good jobs in Jammu and outside the state. Some migrant families have taken loans from their friends/relatives/banks (wherever possible) and sold their immovable properties in Kashmir (mostly as distress sales). With this money some people have been able to buy house plots/flats etc. in Jammu, Delhi and elsewhere. Also some of the parents have been somehow garnering resources to finance the higher professional education of their children, when opportunities arise, as an investment for children's secure future - a top priority in the scheme of things of the community.

This description of the situation sounds fine as far as it goes but in a very limited context. First of all thousands of KP migrants who came later or due to some administrative reasons or because of their movement from one place to another failed to get themselves registered as migrants. Thus they remain deprived of the benefits of the relief measures stated above. Besides, the improvements achieved in the camps have followed many years of hard struggle. The J&K state government has sometimes been harsh and insensitive to their-genuine grievances. Some years back an absolutely peaceful procession of KPs while proceeding towards the residence of the then Chief Minister, Farooq Abdullah, at Jammu, was so brutally lathi-charged by the police that many members were severely wounded and some had their bones broken ending up as handicapped persons for life. This is one example of arrogant brute force being wantonly used against peaceful citizens asking for some improvement in their troubled lives in the camps.

However, these things apart, the real, the very basic issues lie elsewhere - in Kashmir Valley. These pertain to the very complex matters woven into the action of the abandonment of homes under circumstances where the state found itself powerless in coming to the rescue of the peaceful citizen. We shall deal with this subject in the next chapter.

CHAPTER – 12

VIOLENCE IN KASHMIR: CONTEXT AND PRETEXT

Homo sapiens is the most violent of species on the earth. No other species — none whatsoever — can even remotely match the human proclivity and capability to destroy and kill one's own with impunity and for a thousand and one reasons - culturally invented - need for basic resources, religion, colonisation, nationalism, destruction of hostile regimes, establishment of peace, etc. Apparently the concept and thought of violence is embedded in the genetic code of Homo sapiens. Look at the historical evidence of the millions being killed during numerous conflicts, especially, the last two world wars, and all major violent situations that have followed these. No wonder then that the great thinkers and leaders of humankind, like Buddha, Ashoka, Christ, Gandhi and many others, across the ages, felt the need to preach peace and non-violence in human affairs to wean humankind away from its violent ways and tendencies for the good of its own destiny and the well-being of all other living beings on this earth. But we have a long way to go yet to follow this path.

This was a basic thought at the back of our minds, but let us return to recent historical developments in Kashmir. We know that Kashmir's history is replete with wars, civil strife, invasions, and all that. But the hundred years of Dogra rule in Jammu and Kashmir under the paramount power of the British rule in India, had been an era of very peaceful existence for the people, especially in Kashmir Valley. In fact, even violent crimes involving murders, revenge killings, and dacoities were rare. But this idyllic scene was rudely shattered with the Pakistan's invasion of Jammu and Kashmir State on October 22, 1947, initially with irregular 'tribal' forces soon followed by regular Pakistani army. Thus was laid the basis for a period of political turmoil, major wars - and in the last two decades, growth of militancy and terrorism in Kashmir leading to endless all-round strife and violence. The exodus of about three lakh Kashmiri Pandits in 1990, and later, is a direct off-shoot of these developments. This violence and strife are a gift of Pakistan to Kashmir, as she has actively instigated, organised, guided and financed the long term violence and proxy war there with the sole objective of annexing the state as part of its own territory. But Kashmiris have had a heavy price to pay for Pakistan's greed and ulterior motives. Of course, the slogans and banners proclaim their support for the cause of "freedom struggle" of Kashmiris. The proxy war has been pursued through the concept and instrument of the "Islamic Jehad". We shall return to this point a little later.

Jammu and Kashmir state unfortunately has remained in the eye of the storm since 1947 even before the Maharaja of Kashmir had signed the instrument of accession with the Indian Union in October 1947. The invasion of the State by Pakistan forces had already taken place. The India-Pakistan war of 1947-48 led to a ceasefire under UN auspices after India took the matter to UN Security Council. About one third of the State territory has remained under Pakistan's occupation since. The ceasefire line was renamed Line of Control (LOC) after the 1971 India-Pakistan war. In the UN and other international forums many western powers encouraged Pakistan to act in an intransigent manner. This attitude received further impetus from China's close friendship with Pakistan in the years following the India-China war of 1962. In fact, China managed to formally annex part of the state's territory in Pakistan occupied Kashmir through an agreement with Pakistan. According to the Pakistani line of propaganda "Kashmir was a disputed territoiy with a dominant Muslim population inclined towards Pakistan but India was maintaining its hold on it because of its military might."

The upshot is that while Jammu & Kashmir State remains a part of the Indian Union like its other constituent states, it has some special features that set it apart from the latter. These are -

(a) It is a Muslim majority state with borders touching Pakistan and China and part of its original territory is illegally occupied by Pakistan and also by China.

(b) It has been under international gaze and attention being on the UN agenda as a "dispute" between two member States (for half a century now).

(c) It has also been on the agenda of the organization of Islamic countries on Pakistan's request.

(d) With the loss of East Pakistan after it gained an independent status as a state named Bangladesh in 1971, Pakistan has become ever more intent upon annexing Kashmir Valley to its own territory. The Kargil war in 1999 was one cruder attempt to achieve this goal.

(e) Ever since 1947 the Pakistan's official media have been directing towards Kashmiri people venomous propaganda against Hindustan and Hindus.

(f) This work has also been carried through the network of Pakistan oriented Muslim religious clergy in mosques and *'madrasas'* in Kashmir over the years.

While Pakistan had been indulging in activities of its choice regarding Jammu and Kashmir State the effort on the Indian side has been all along to help develop an economically backward state, riven with war and strife, with growth in various sectors for which potential and demand existed. In the field of education, for instance, remarkable progress has been registered since 1947 with new schools and colleges and professional institutions in agriculture, engineering, medicine etc. Two universities are functioning in Srinagar (Kashmir University) and Jammu (Jammu University) and a third one an agriculture university at Sopore. The state had no university of its own before 1947.

The spread of education at all levels created a huge demand for jobs for the educated youth — much more than the state could take care of. The rising unemployment created resentment and disenchantment. There have also been complaints of widespread corruption among the politicians and government officials with no effective avenues for redress of grievances because the political parties in the State were alleged to be routinely using corrupt practices to gain and remain in power. The heady combination of greater awareness and understanding of local issues and wider problems and deep anger over the flavour of corruption in vital areas of life - in the background of the Pakistani propaganda, instigation and support - led to the growth of militancy in Kashmir in the mid-eighties. It had a fair degree of support among the youth especially in the urban centres. At that time an outfit called JKLF (Jammu and Kashmir Liberation Front) was the main organization leading the insurgency. Soon the militancy became violent and metamorphosed into terrorism. In Pakistan Occupied Kashmir and Pakistan's Punjab, terrorist camps were opened and training facilities provided. Besides, lots and lots of money flowed in through illegal channels to 'terrorist cells' in the state to finance the operations of destruction and mayhem. Thus the anger and frustrations of the local people which should have found expression and redress through democratic channels was hijacked by Pakistan to give it a "*jehadi* face". At a later stage Pakistan took nearly complete control of the "terrorist operations" by sending its own terrorist warriors to Kashmir as commanders and *mujahideens* of variously named outfits. The local recruits, if any, had to mostly work under their orders, directions and guidance.

The targets of the terrorists were government officials, police and other security forces and Kashmiri Pandits and other non-Muslims. Large numbers of KPs were killed between January and July 1990 in the Valley and thousands of letters and notices were despatched to KP families threatening their womenfolk with kidnappings and worse. Notices with death threats were also nailed to trees in the villages against KP men.

However, by 1995 things had considerably quietened down and peace had returned to the Valley as the local support to militancy and terrorism had tapered off. At this stage Pakistan injected lots of highly trained terrorist leaders mostly of Pakistani origin to regroup and command the "weak and indifferent Kashmiri militants" to renew the violence and mayhem against local targets including de-motivated militants.

Terrorism is a cannibalistic mother; it kills and devours its children. According to Govt. of India figures, till 2001, about 28,000 Kashmiris (Muslims) had been killed in the insurgency. Of these 9800 were by the terrorists themselves.

The Muslims greet each other with the words "Salaam-alaikum" meaning "peace be upon you". To kill the innocent and helpless is strictly forbidden in Islam. But the jehadi terrorists in their obsession with their creed of violence "stretch and refine" their outlandish arguments to create "a domain of validity" for their own activities, however abhorrent these may seem to the wider world.

The violence in Kashmir against the KPs is not merely physical i.e., killing of some people and destruction of their properties. Kashmiri Pandits are an important segment of the traditional Kashmiri society. Their exodus has meant dismembering the Kashmiri Society and vulgarising and demeaning Kashmiri culture, history and politics, (see Pandit, T. N.: 2003: 175-188).

A community may use various devices and means within its cultural traditions to maintain its identity but for this purpose it has to maintain a network of stable relationships -

(A) Within the community.

(B) With other communities within the fold of the larger society.

(C) With the natural environment

(D) With the supernatural forces impinging on its destiny in powerful and mysterious ways.

Kashmiri Pandits in the Valley, though, not a very large population, were spread out across the districts, tehsils and villages and towns of Kashmir. Each village or area had its own oral history, local tales, special geographical features, very special holy places, many times near natural springs, streams etc. Even in small hamlets or villages neighbourhood relations (sometimes based also on lineage affiliations) were most vital. Marriages were arranged across distant settlements. So the community was truly linked up through these relationships across long distances in the Valley.

All settlements in the Valley had local Muslim communities living alongside KPs. With these a whole network of economic and social relations existed that were suffused with a feeling of mutual benefit and camaraderie. All over Kashmir Valley there are well known holy places held sacred by Hindus and KPs, which are part of their centuries old tradition and folklore. Pilgrimages to these places were greatly valued and desired.

KPs have made enormous contributions to the literary, artistic and aesthetic traditions of Kashmir. When in 1989-90 Kashmiri Pandits were forced to leave their homes in the Valley on a mass scale, violence was done to all these relationships and cherished traditions at one go. In a way it was "assassination" of a whole Community (Pandits) and disfigurement of a whole Society (all Kashmiris). The quality and flavour of the life that was cannot be resurrected ever. This is the real damage the terrorists have done to Kashmir.

Earlier we talked of human obsession with violence of all kinds under various pretexts. But TERRORISM is the worst kind of violence that humankind has invented. According to Salman Rushdie: "Terrorism is not the pursuit of legitimate complaints by illegitimate means. The terrorist wraps himself in the world's grievances to cloak his true motives. Whatever the killers are trying to achieve it seems improbable that building a better world is part of it. The fundamentalist seeks to down a great deal more than buildings. Such people are against freedom of speech, a multi-party political system, universal adult suffrage, accountable government, women's rights, pluralism, secularism, short skirts, dancing, beardlessness, evolution theory, sex. These are tyrants, not Muslims..."

(reproduced in The Times of India of 29.08.2005 from The Guardian, London).

Let us pray that peace returns to Kashmir soon enough so that we can all see that happen. Let us endeavour in whatever ways we can - to contribute towards the achievement of that noble objective. That will be our gift to the coming generations in Kashmir, India and Pakistan.

CHAPTER – 13

IMPORTANT HIGHLIGHTS

Ch. 1. Research Matters

Topic: To study Kashmiri Pandit Migrants as victims of conflict and violence with special reference to their women and children.

Universe: Kashmiri Pandits living in Delhi, Jammu and Kashmir.

Sample: 743 households with a population of 4000 (2083 males and 1917 females). The break up is; Delhi 250 households (population 1277), Jammu 340 households, (population 1706) and Kashmir 153 households (population 1017).

Methods: The households were selected at random mostly within the migrant camps in various parts of Delhi and Jammu and those in Kashmir were from towns and villages across the Valley.

A comprehensive schedule (questionnaire) was used for collecting quantitative data on Demography, Education, Employment, and Economic matters (losses of property and new acquisitions etc.). Their views were recorded regarding causes of migration, general conditions and future prospects etc. Trained investigators visited each household personally and did their work under the guidance of local coordinators and the Principal Project Coordinator.

Fieldwork was done during the months of October 2002 to March 2003. Tabulation of data was done in 2003 under the supervision of Principal Project Coordinator who also analysed the quantitative and qualitative data in early 2004.

The Principal Project Coordinator completed the writing of the report in December 2004.

Ch. 2. Demography

In our sample half the population is in the 0-19 (24%) and 40-59 (26%) age group. About 2/5 population is in the 20-39 (38%) age groups. The above 60 groups (12%) comprised 1/8 of the total population.

There are on the average 920 females per thousand males against the figures 933 (India) 900 (J and K State) and 914 (Kashmir Valley) as per 2001 census.

The 0-6 children's population in the sample is only 7.5% which is about half of the figures for Kashmir Valley (15.8%) J and K State (14.2%) and India *(15. 4%) 2001* census.

The low figures at this level indicate low fertility in the population. This could be due to disturbance of normal life after migration, poor health conditions (mental and physical) and total lack of privacy in one-room tents and flats, etc. Besides, the above factors could induce a policy of deliberately avoiding having more kids because of poor living conditions and low incomes.

Ch. 3. Literacy and Education

Kashmiri Pandits constitute one of the most advanced communities in terms of literacy and education. The facts and figures in our sample reflect this reality.

The overall literacy rate is 89% while for males it is 97% and for females 81%. The older women coming from the villages have not had access to schools etc. For J and K comparative rates are 54.5% (persons) 65.7% (males) and 41.8% (females) in 2001 census.

As far as the levels of education achieved, here also the figures are much better for males. In any case the overall figures are like this -

(a) Class 10/12 38.2%

(b) B. A. and more 25.2%

(c) B. Sc. and Tech, degrees 12. 3%

In professional education 67% males against 33% females are qualified in Delhi and Jammu. But in Kashmir only 25% females have these qualifications against 75% males.

Ch. 4. Employment Pattern

In the job market, women remain highly discriminated against. Also, the overall employment situation is not very bright for the KP migrants. It is 33% in Delhi and 22% in Jammu. In Kashmir it is a little better at 34%. But against 52% males employed in Delhi, only 13% females are working. The figures for Jammu are 37.5% and 5% and for Kashmir 52% and 13% respectively. The eamer/dependent ratio is 3.0 in Delhi, 4.5 in Jammu (due to lesser jobs) and 3.0 in Kashmir. The overall average is 3.5. Also there is high incidence of under employment and unstable (purely private, insecure, low-salaried) jobs.

Ch. 5. State of Health

The data for this chapter was collected under two heads:

(A) **Death:** Number and causes of death of members who had died between 1990 (year of exodus) and 2002 (year of field work).

(B) **Disease:** the health problems of the living populations.

The above data were collected region-wise and tabulated sex-wise and age-wise.

(A) **Death:** The ratio of deaths to surviving population ranges from 8.8% in Delhi and 7.5% in Kashmir (data collected for comparison) while at Jammu it is 8.0%. The major causes of death have been depression, heart disease, paralysis, cancer, diabetes and sunstroke, in Delhi and Jammu. In Kashmir, besides cancer and heart disease, bronchitis and gastric disease are major killers. Death rates are highest in the 60+ age groups i.e. 76% in Delhi, 64% in Jammu and 72% in Kashmir. The death rate declines appreciably as we go down to lower age grades. No deaths are reported in the 0-14 age groups except 3 cases of deaths caused by accidents in Jammu. The ratio of deaths between males and females is 3 : 2 in Delhi and Kashmir. But at Jammu numbers of deaths are somewhat evenly matched between males and females: 51.5% and 48.5%.

(B) **Disease:** The data covers only Delhi and Jammu samples. The major diseases suffered by the living population are diabetes, *depression, heart problems, hypertension, bronchitis, gastric* problems and arthritis etc. But here again it is mostly in the higher age groups (45-59 and 60 plus) that the major health problems occur. This is the case both in Delhi and Jammu. The 0-14 and 15-29 age groups seem to be in a good state of health.

Ch. 6. Path of Reconstruction

After all the economic damage and destruction there has been a serious effort at reconstructing house and hearth. The obvious indications are the land, house, and items of material culture as aids to a pleasanter life. A look at the

Table below is useful:

Item	Delhi	Jammu
1) House/flat	72.0%	10.0%
2) House plot	15.6%	09.6%
3) Phone	71.0%	24.0%
4) Refrigerators	83.0%	69.0%
5) Television	92.0%	85.0%
6) Washing machine	48.0%	08.0%
7) Car/scooter	36.0%	12.0%

Obviously, Delhi group is doing much better because of better opportunities (in a metropolis), better education and better employment. Also, because about 16.8% households in our sample are pre-1989 migrants, whereas in our Jammu sample it is much less, 8.8%. The latter have had lot more time to establish themselves in a new place.

Ch. 7. Property Losses

The migrant Kashmiri Pandits have left behind their big houses, shops, agricultural and horticultural lands, household goods, goods for sale in shops, cattle, trees and also their neighbourhood and social life and their beloved land of Kashmir.

The losses only in material terms can be counted household-wise. In Jammu it comes to Rs. 22.7 lakhs and in Delhi Rs. 10.4 lakhs per household. In our opinion the figures are underestimated in terms of present market value. Even in Kashmir Valley Kashmiri Pandits have suffered losses, which average Rs. 1.6 lakhs per household.

Ch. 8. Agony of Women and Children

The uprooting of a community causes maximum suffering to the most vulnerable sections i.e., women and children. We have listed the recorded killings of 40 women (including unmarried young girls). But many more young girls have been kidnapped and/or raped in the countryside. There is one reported case of a young girl being raped in front of her family members in Anantnag district.

Destruction of home and hearth and the death of dear ones and then the task of rebuilding and reconstructing one's life puts a very heavy burden on womenfolk, both mentally and physically. The Kashmiri Pandit women have come out with flying colours in discharge of their responsibility and in playing a most constructive role in gathering up the lost strands of life. But half of their population is paying a price for this in terms of mental stress and tension, depression and other ailments, in the absence of required level of medical care.

Then there has been the difficult job of making readjustments in a new place and new people under stressful conditions. The children's worst nightmare has been loss of good schools and friends and home conditions. The migrant schools started initially in tents minus fans, minus basic equipment, minus any drinking water and toilets, in the terrible heat and dust of a Jammu or Delhi summer, were little hellholes. Thank God that phase is now over and they are attending normal schools now.

Ch. 9. Nadimarg Massacre

There have been several incidents of major mass killings of non-Muslims at the hands of terrorists since 1990. Nadimarg massacre is one of the most gruesome of these incidents - occurred on March 23, 2003. In this incident 24 KPs living in Nadimarg village were called out from their houses at night, lined up and gunned down. Among the dead were 13 males of whom two were teen aged boys, two were 2 year-old babies in their young mothers' arms. Among the eleven females were 5 unmarried girls and two young wives, all below 30 years of age. The incident received national and international publicity but none was caught or punished for the crime.

Ch. 10. Random Cases: Some Concise Statements

In this chapter we have some brief statements made by our informants and recorded in 31 of our schedules (questionnaires) selected at random. The statements convey the reactions to the ground realities vitally affecting the lives of the migrants. They bring us close to the minds of the migrants and impart a touch of authenticity and reality to our report. We have offered these here without comment.

To protect the identity of the informants and their families we have used only serial numbers and code numbers for the schedules.

Ch. 11. Relief and Rehabilitation

Following the exodus of KPs from the Valley in 1990 the relief work at Jammu, and Delhi (and elsewhere) was done on an emergency basis by the J&K Government supported by the Central Government. Initial accommodation provided was in tents, community halls, etc. The conditions were pretty unsatisfactory initially but gradually there was improvement. Tents were replaced by single rooms (work on 2 room apartment is on). The cash allowance per family of 4 and above has been raised to Rs. 3000/- from Rs. 2400/-. Better schools and medical facilities and roads and transport to camps and shops for daily necessities have come up near the campsites.

Also, government employees in service continue to draw their normal salaries (and also pension on reaching retirement age) without joining any post of duty away from Kashmir Valley.

However, the excruciating pain of being very far away both physically and figuratively from their real homes remains deep in their hearts.

Ch. 12. Violence in Kashmir: Context and Pretext

In this chapter there is brief recall of events that led to the growth of militancy and terrorism in Kashmir. That a peaceful and peace loving people were thrust into war, violence and mayhem has been a gift of Pakistan to Kashmir. Pakistan pushed the Islamic jehadi elements to "liberate Kashmir" from "Hindus and Hindustan" by hijacking the local discontent and giving it a jehadi face. In the process thousands of innocent as well as misguided Kashmiri people got killed, thousands were wounded and maimed, thousands lost their homes.

Violence is indeed a human failing but terrorism is its ugliest face. We need to reject it outright and return Kashmir to peaceful conditions for the development and well being of her people and the people of the Indian subcontinent.

REFERENCES

1. Bamzai, P N K	1994	Cultural and Political History of Kashmir, Vol. I, New Delhi.
2. Census of India	2001	Provisional Population Tables, Paper 2001 Supplementary
3. Grover, Virender	1996	The Story of Kashmir Yesterday and Today, Vol. II, New Delhi.
4. Jagmohan	1992	My Frozen Turbulence in Kashmir (second edition), New Delhi.
5. Pandit, S L	1999	My Kashmir Diary, New Delhi.
6. Pandit, TN	2004	"Kashmiriyat an Anthropological Viewpoint" in Kashmir and Its People, MK Kaw (ed), New Delhi.
7. Raina, ML	2004	Kashmir Documents, New Delhi
8. Rushdie, Salman	2005	Report in The Times of India, New Delhi, dt. 29.08.2005 (reproduced from The Guardian, London)
9. Sidhwa, Shiraz	1996	Militant Viewpoint in (745-51 p.) in V. Grover (ed). The story of Kashmir Yesterday and Today Vol. II, New Delhi.

APPENDIX

AIKS meets Sushma Choudhary, J and K Govt, asked to get encroachments on Pandits' properties vacated

[Note: Various Kashmiri Pandit organizations, have been making representations from time to time to Jammu and Kashmir Government and Government of India, drawing attention to the problems being faced by the KP Migrants. Also, they have been conveying their opinions on the broader issues related to J and K State and future of Kashmiri Pandits. All India Kashmiri Samaj (AIKS) one of the most prominent of these organisations has of late, been doing this work in a very systematic and mature manner. Here we have reproduced an article on this subject published by them in Naad, Vol. XIV, No. 2 (Feb. 2006) p. 6, which is useful reading.]

New Delhi

The high powered inter-ministerial group constituted by the Union Government for the rehabilitation of displaced Kashmiri Pandits has asked the J and K Govt, to devise immediate mechanism to vacate encroachments of properties of Kashmir Pandits in the Valley. The govt has been asked to prepare an inventory of property of displaced Kashmiri Pandits and put it on the website at the earliest. This information was given by the chairperson of the group, Ms. Sushma Choudhary to a delegation of AIKS, which had a two-hour long meeting with her here on 22nd Jan., 2005. The delegation led by the president of the Samaj, Sh. M. K. Kaw sought confidence building measures along with constitutional guarantees ensuring political, social and economic rights of the displaced community before any dialogue with the representatives of AIKS is initiated by the govt, on the return of KPs back to their homes. Sharing the concern over the plight of the displaced community,

Ms. Choudhary agreed to recommend regularization of employees including teachers in Delhi and other parts of the country. The convenor of the high power group also promised to recommend an ordinance for the upkeep and management of Kashmiri Pandit shrines and places of worship and return of management control of minority educational institutions including the Gandhi Memorial College, back to the Pandits. The delegation made a detailed presentation for the short and long term rehabilitation of KPs. The highlights are:

Education and Culture

- The committee should order the survey of camp and non-camp Kashmiri refugees to have a database about the present status of educational scenario, with remedial measures to eliminate dropout rate.
- Four Kendriya Vidyalayas, already sanctioned by the Ministry of Human Resource Development for the camps in Jammu province and Delhi, should be made functional on a time bound basis.
- The committee should recommend reservation for Kashmiri refugee students in the educational institutions, both professional and non professional till their return to their homes or at least for a minimum period of ten years.
- The committee should set up an AIKS Educational Fund with an initial corpus of Rs. 50 crore from the government.
- The committee should restore the management and control of Kashmiri Pandit minority institutions back to the community and with a comprehensive financial package for their facelift and infrastructural development.
- The committee should recommend setting up of "Sharda Peeth" university in Jammu and Kashmir. The proposed university will not only focus on excellence in the field of modern higher education, but also establish chairs in the names of Kalhana, Abhinav Gupta, Shri Bhat, Badshah and many others to preserve the rich cultural and literary treasure of Kashmir.

- To preserve the roots of Kashmiri refugees, the committee should recommend the restoration of Devanagari as an additional alternate script to Kashmiri language.
- For the setting up of a Centre for Kashmir Studies in New Delhi, the committee should recommend allocation of at least Rs. 10 crores to the Kashmir Education, Culture and Science Society, Delhi. The magazines WAAKH, Naad, Aalav, Kshirbhawani Times, and others need immediate patronage for projecting the plural Kashmiri thought.
- The committee should recommend the enactment of a law for the management of Hindu shrines in the Valley by Kashmiri Pandits themselves, on SGPC pattern.

Housing, Rehabilitation and Return

- Top priority to be accorded to 700 KPs still living in the Valley.
- The two room flats, presently known as two room tenements scheme, should be constructed on a war footing.
- The flats should be constructed in locations separate from the camp areas. The dwelling units should be in a properly planned and laid-out housing colonies with all basic facilities of roads, drinking water, electricity, playgrounds, auditoria, parks, proper transportation and schooling facilities.
- These flats should have a *puja* room, kitchen, and bathroom apart from the two living rooms of large dimensions to accommodate families.
- The scheme of flats must include those refugees who are paying rents which can be ill-afforded by them. Also, the registration should be open to those refugees who could not register themselves with authorities due to one or the other reason and include them also in the ambit of housing scheme.
- Persons whose properties have been looted and damaged should be paid same compensation as paid in cases of fire. Revenue authorities must make an inventory of all such properties and notify the same.

- Government must prepare a white paper giving full description of the properties taken over by it for safe custody. The same must be recorded and details must be published.
- The Government must issue necessary instructions to insurance companies to accept all kinds of left out properties of refugees as insurable properties.
- For rehabilitation of displaced persons still living in the Valley the two room flats should be constructed in erstwhile predominantly Kashmiri Pandit areas like Jawahar Nagar, Raj Bagh, Karan Nagar, Habba Kadal, Indra. Nagar, Barzullah in Srinagar district and respective district headquarters in other districts.
- Recovery of all housing loans drawn by Government employees should be waived off as they lost the houses for which such loans were taken.
- Revenue records as on 19/20 January 1990 must be frozen and kept under safe custody. No mutation must be allowed. All sales of land and other properties by the Pandits should be declared as "Distress Sales" and be declared as null and void.
- The one-room flats allotted to some refugees by DDA in Delhi on hire purchase basis should be given to them free of cost till their return to the Valley.

For a long term permanent rehabilitation and return, a safe and secure environment in the Valley is a must. Kashmiri Pandits will return to their homes in the Valley in wholesale, not in driblets and when the security environment is conducive. No decision on the return should be taken without detailed deliberations with AIKS. Also, the majority community organizations must take initiatives to invite Kashmiri Pandits to a life of dignity and honour with full constitutional guarantees of their civil, political and economic rights. For that an inter community debate must precede the return.

Long-term measures are as under:

- Involvement of Kashmiri Pandits in the ongoing dialogue process.

- Evolution of a mechanism to have the state Chief Minister on a rotational basis from all the regions/faiths. This will usher in the real democratic and secular polity in the state giving recognition to all regions and groups, including Kashmiri Pandits.
- Devolution of powers to any of the state's institutions only after discussing with representatives of all regions and faiths including the Pandits. With the present arrangement, Kashmiri Pandits have suffered, with our population plummeting from 4% in 1947 to 0.01% in 2001.
- Political space for Pandits with adequate representation in parliament and state assembly with representation in the J and K, and Union cabinets.
- Safeguard of economic, social and political rights of Pandits through mandatory constitutional amendments to that effect. Passing a legislation for consolidation and management by the KPs of all their shrines, places of worship and properties appurtenant thereto.
- Extension of healing touch policy to KPs and return of management and control of minority educational institutions back to the community.
- Declaration of Kashmiri Pandits as a reverse minority and declaring them as Internally Displaced People till they return.
- Removal of all encroachments from properties belonging to Kashmiri Pandits.
- Any transfer of immovable property like houses, agricultural land, orchards etc should be cancelled and declared null and void as "Distress Sale".
- Such transferred properties must be restored back to original owners. In any case, if this is not possible the original owner must be given a suitable alternate piece of land and a suitable financial package for construction of house.
- A massive package for reconstruction of depleted, terrorist damaged, worn out and burnt houses belonging to the Pandits. The entire financial liability should be borne by the Government. Sending the Pandits back to their homes should be a deferred option.

Economic Rehabilitation

- To set up an economic foundation for the welfare and economic upliftment of the community, with an initial corpus of Rs. 1000 crores by the Government. A representative of the Union Home Ministry may be included to supervise the utilization of this fund which will be managed by AIKS.
- A separate head is sought in the state and central government budgets for the relief and rehabilitation of Kashmiri Pandits. The central and state governments must reserve at least 10% of all jobs for Kashmiri Pandits with age relaxation of at least 10 years.
- A special recruitment drive in paramilitary forces and defence services for Kashmiri Pandits with age relaxation of at least 10 years.
- Financial and employment avenues under various schemes of GOI like IRDP, SEUY and KV1C should be extended to unemployed, educated and uneducated Kashmiri refugee youth with age relaxation of at least 10 years.
- Creation of a two-tier consultative apparatus by having a Committee under the Home Minister and the other under the CM, with AIKS representatives, so that all matters pertaining to the community are dealt with in consultation with the accredited representatives of the community.
- Increase in the amount of relief provided to Kashmiri Pandit refugees to be related with the price index and revised accordingly. Amount of relief to be made uniform across states.
- Registered migrants to be permitted to transfer registration from one place to another in the event of change of their address.
- Displaced Government employees to be treated as on duty and paid all entitlements till they retire or resume duties at their places of work.
- All pension cases and those relating to final payments of GPF/CPF must be settled as a time bound programme. In the event of non-settlement of such cases within the pre-fixed deadlines, the amounts claimed by the employees should be paid to them on collateral evidence.

- Kashmiri refugees should be exempt from payment of Income Tax on all incomes accruing or arising within the state or outside till their return. For this, the migrant registration certificate from revenue authorities should be considered as their identity.
- Soft loans for setting up income generating units must be announced without asking for collateral securities. These loans should be secured by only individual guarantees of the borrowers. Alternatively, group guarantees could be considered.
- Allottees of temporary shops or vending sites in Delhi and other parts to be provided formal tehbazari status and infrastructural facilities like electricity and municipal identities to enable them to make their livelihood without harassment from various agencies.
- Loans outstanding against refugee traders, entrepreneurs, agriculturists and all other categories must be waived off or paid by the Government.
- Government should compensate Kashmiri Pandits for loss of income from their economic assets which have been usurped by anti-social elements.
- All arrears of Income tax, Sales tax, Excise, and other statutory dues from Kashmiri Pandits should be waived off.
- Remaining amounts against ex-gratia payments of relief, which have been only partly paid to Pandits should be released to the affected families.
- Regularisation of employees including teachers working in NCT of Delhi, J and K and other states as ad hoc employees.

Health Sector

- Issuance of a Health card on pattern of CGHS to enable the displaced community to avail proper health care. Till issuance of such cards, Migrant ration cards should be treated as Health cards. Health insurance cover to all Pandit refugees. The premiums must be paid by the Government.
- Persons holding such health cards must be entertained without any charge by designated private hospitals in whole of the country, especially the specialty hospitals for designated diseases.

- One time grant of Rs. 10.00 crores to existing Relief Fund of AIKS for emergency medical care of patients suffering from fatal ailments like cancer, kidney failures, cardiac and neurological diseases. A nominee of the Government to supervise the disbursement out of the said fund.
- Dispensaries and hospitals with modern diagnostic facilities be set up at all migrant camps in Jammu and Delhi.
- Immediate closure of polluting and hazardous industrial units near existing camps. A case to cite is the cement plant near Batarbalian camp at Udhampur. Correspondence with relevant authorities has been of no avail.

All these points were discussed in detail in the meeting and Ms. Sushma Choudhary assured the AIKS delegation that she will incorporate most of the points raised by the apex body. The other members of the delegation included Sh. M. L. Matto, Vice President AIKS, Central Zone, based in Mumbai, General Secretary AIKS Sh. H. L. Wangnoo, Political Advisor Sh. Shiban Dudha, President KCSS Sh. Nanji Raina, Joint Secretary AIKS Sh. Vinod Pandita. This was the second meeting of AIKS with the high power inter-ministerial group.

Prior to the visit of the group to the camps in Jammu and Udhampur, the AIKS President had a preliminary discussion with Ms. Choudhary. The recommendations for the rehabilitation of KP Community in exile have been given in tune with the points discussed at the two day global conclave of Kashmiri Pandits at Bangalore last month.

A project financially supported by

The Ministry of Human Resources Development, Department of Women and Child Development, Government of India

INDEX